Who Am I?

Self-Actualization for Followers of Jesus

Wim Codington

Wim Codington

Cover art by Brian Hayden

With editorial help from Elsbeth Codington, Libby Codington, Allan Douglas, and Will Ayers.

Scripture quotations are from the ESV® Bible (The Holy Bible, English Standard Version®), copyright 2001 by Crossway, a publishing ministry of Good News Publishers. Used by permission. All rights reserved.

CONTENTS

Introduction	6
Part One: The Essential Human Identity	12
Part Two: Shared Expressions of Identity as Followers of Jesus	38
Ambassador Identity	42
Sojourner Identity	51
Warrior Identity	65
Part Three: Your Unique Expressions of Identity as a Follower of Jesus	88
Expression vs. Essence	91
The Deposit in You	95
Identify the Deposit	101
Cultivate the Deposit	110
Redefining Productivity	116
Redefining Scarcity	127
Embracing Weakness	138
Embracing Foolishness	143

The Final Secret	150
The Final Charge	153
Possible Objections to the Message in This Book	157
Appendix: The Truth and Authority of the Bible	161
Reflection	169
Let Us Talk	171

I do not write these things to make you ashamed, but to admonish you as my beloved children. For though you have countless guides in Christ, you do not have many fathers. For I became your father in Christ Jesus through the gospel. I urge you, then, be imitators of me. (I Corinthians 4:14-16)

I have the lavish privilege of having had at least ten fathers in my life. This book is dedicated to them, for through them I have discovered who I am.

God - He made me, chose me, redeemed me, validated me, affirmed me, and adopted me. I will be His son forever.

Lewis Codington - He taught me grace, humility, how to die, how to live, how to love, and how to pursue. He is more like Jesus than anyone I know.

Jon Homewood - He cared for me with laughter and generosity. He is a courageous and faithful man.

Gareth Wroe - He helped me to take God seriously and not take myself too seriously. He is a leader of leaders.

Kelly Kapic - He saw me, heard me, and blessed me during a season of change. He is able to bear heavy burdens with grace and love.

David Taylor - His gentleness made me great on the battlefield. He taught me how to endure.

Jeff Smith - He taught me how to look past the outside and see the person within. His kindness and understanding are immeasurable.

Sam DeVane - He taught me the power of leading by example, doing and saying the right thing no matter what, offering relational support through sponsorship and endorsement, and getting to the root of a problem with relentless perseverance. He has fathered many people.

Jan Esterline - He helped me understand and experience God's fatherly heart to call forth that which is not, affirm that which is in process, and bless that which is good.

John Piper - He gave me words to express my longings, my yearnings, and my deep desires. He gave me courage to release everything but God and to trust that God will satisfy more than anything else will. He validated my passion.

INTRODUCTION

An ancient question has been given new power to disrupt and challenge existing social norms through the hyper-connectedness enabled by modern technology: Who am I and what is my purpose? With the ability to continuously compare ourselves with others and to control how people perceive us through the images and text that we publicize about ourselves, the question has risen from a whisper reserved for the few wealthy and educated people in the ancient world to a deafening roar that is inescapable every time I open Facebook.

The question has changed my life.

From a young age, I remember thinking to myself, "When I am grown, I am going to change the world. The world is going to be a different place because of me."

Many people can probably relate with that statement or with the desire to have impact.

In my own quest for impact and search to answer the question "What should I do?" I found myself asking an even more foundational question which seemed to contain the key to my desire for impact. The foundational question for me was "Who is Wim Codington?" I had to know myself in order to know how I was supposed to change the world.

For much of my life, this question produced fear, anxiety, and loneliness in me. I did not know myself, and therefore I did not know what I was supposed to do. All I knew was that I wanted to be great, and the only way I knew how to prove my greatness to myself was to endlessly compare myself with others, searching for innumerable ways to demonstrate my superiority.

I was very good in school and achieved high grades all the way through the end of college, completing an impressive degree in business and accounting with two minors tacked on for good measure. I graduated with the highest honors possible.

I competed in college athletics for two years and won an award for "rookie of the year" my first year and "most improved" my second year. I won the cross country home meet my senior year. After college, I ran marathons and won prize money through my running more than once.

I went on to work for one of the most prestigious

professional services companies in the world, predictably rising through the ranks and building a good reputation for myself with my clients, colleagues, and friends. I earned a high salary, gave money away generously, lived in a large house, made good financial choices, volunteered in my community, was recognized an exemplary father to my children and a loving husband to my wife.

I was great.

This continual cycle of striving to be great and comparing myself with others achieved a measure of greatness for me to enjoy. It turned a few heads and raised a few eyebrows (which is what I wanted to happen), and it gave me the thrill of feeling great... for a moment. However, inevitably two negative things happened very predictably because of this cycle.

First, the thrill of the greatness ended. Each time I achieved something good and sought to multiply the greatness by comparing myself (in my own mind and sometimes even vocally with others), the good thing was eventually forgotten, and the thrill faded. The uncertainty about my own greatness and my identity came back. Who am I? I needed yet another chance to prove myself.

Second, the cycle of comparison cost me close relationships. Who wants to keep company with someone that is consumed with their own greatness? There are few things more putrid. I found that my relationships with friends and family stagnated or declined. I found that my 8 younger siblings spent more time with one another than with me.

Fear, anxiety, and loneliness were the inevitable results of this way of thinking and living. I did not know myself any better, and I did not seem to be making any real progress in achieving greatness.

I have come to appreciate the word "authenticity" recently, and it is a favorite word of my generation, the millennial generation. Authenticity is the true essence of something. The desire to know one's true self can also be described as a desire for authenticity.

In addition to the desire for authenticity, a companion desire of many in my generation is for self-actualization. This term, used by Abraham Maslow in his social theory "hierarchy of needs,"[1] represents the final fulfillment of human existence which can only occur after all other more basic needs are met. Google dictionary defines "self-actualization" as "the realization or fulfillment of one's talents and potentialities, especially considered as a drive or need present in everyone."

The term "self-actualization" has been popularized in recent years. Popularization of terms and phrases introduces the danger of loss of meaning. So, it is helpful to define the term for the sake of clarity. To expand on the google definition, I would like to define "self-actualization" as ***the removal of all known barriers to understanding and expressing one's full authentic self***.

Reflecting on my own life story, and comparing mine with the stories of others, it has become clear to me that this searching for identity and purpose in our life stories is a common experience.

Who am I? What is my purpose? What is the meaning of my life? What am I supposed to do with my life?

These are questions that millions of people are asking.

Millions of people are striving to achieve things and to appear successful and happy. This is what we see in the endless stream of Facebook posts, Instagram images, clever tweets, and other online declarations of happiness.

I cannot say with certainty what prompts a person to post a smiling selfie and a message about being happy, and I do not believe for a moment that all assertions of happiness are fake. However, the continuous stream of images and assertions has a familiar feel to me, because it reminds me of my own cycle of searching, striving, achieving, comparing, declaring, forgetting, wondering, searching, striving....

Is this all I am? Is this all I was made for?

In my searching, I have found answers to my own questions about identity and purpose that have enabled courage instead of fear, peace instead of anxiety, and friendship instead of loneliness. The courage, peace, and friendship I have found are abiding and abundant, in stark contrast with the thrill I found from my own accomplishments which invariably evaporated like a morning mist.

The purpose of this book is to provide a framework for every human being to understand who he or she is authentically and how to achieve self-actualization.

I want to share with you the pathway to abiding courage, peace, and friendship so that you too can have abundant life.

First, there is someone you should meet.

PART ONE: THE ESSENTIAL HUMAN IDENTITY

The Original Person

Meet God.

Before the beginning of time, God is.

In the beginning there was no time, so there was no past. Only present. Only God.

God is and has always been perfect and complete, not lacking in anything, having no needs or deficiencies.

He is infinitely good, wise, just, and powerful.

He is also infinitely loving.

God's transcendent perfection and beauty in all of its wonderful qualities can be summed up in one word: glory.

Before the beginning of time and space, when only God was (is), out of His infinite wisdom and love, God spoke. Words with the power to communicate His infinite glory and to create something out of nothing flowed from His mouth.

He made everything that can be seen and known and experienced, and He made many things that have not yet been discovered. He made it all perfect and good, as an expression of His own glory.

God's greatest creation was human beings. Into human beings He placed expressions of His own nature that He did not place in other created things or beings.

Only of human beings did God say we were created in His own image and to have dominion over the rest of creation:

> *Then God said, "Let us make man **in our image, after our likeness**. And **let them have dominion** over the fish of the sea and over the birds of the heavens and over the livestock and over all the earth and over every creeping thing that creeps on the earth." So God created man in his own image, in the image of God he created him; male and female he created them.* (Genesis 1:26-27, emphasis added)[2]

Only of human beings did God say we were crowned with glory and honor in our dominion over all created things:

> *When I look at your heavens, the work of your fingers, the moon and the stars, which you have set in place, what is man that you are mindful of him, and the son of man that you care for him?* ***Yet you have made him a little lower than the heavenly beings and crowned him with glory and honor. You have given him dominion*** *over the works of your hands; you have put all things under his feet, all sheep and oxen, and also the beasts of the field, the birds of the heavens, and the fish of the sea, whatever passes along the paths of the seas.* (Psalm 8:3-8, emphasis added)

Only of human beings did God, through the words of His Son Jesus, say we are of much greater value than other created things (birds and fish):

> *Look at the birds of the air: they neither sow nor reap nor gather into barns, and yet your heavenly Father feeds them.* ***Are you not of more value than they?*** (Matthew 6:26, emphasis added)

And

> *Are not two sparrows sold for a penny? And not one of them will fall to the ground apart from your Father. But even the hairs of your head are all numbered. Fear not, therefore;* ***you are of more value than many sparrows***. (Matthew

10:29-31, emphasis added)

So, God is the original Person, and human value and beauty were created by God as an expression of God's transcendent beauty, or glory. Human beings are the crowning creation among God's many creations.

Human Identity as God-originated

What does all this have to do with discovering my personal identity?

The first step in self-discovery is God-discovery. I am not original. That is, I am not foundational or primary. Only God is original. I was created. I was produced. I was fashioned by a Master Creator who had my particular design in His mind before He even lifted a finger and spoke a word.

Understanding our identity as related to and emanating out of God's identity does not decrease our own value. It does not diminish our dignity or worth. Rather, it establishes our value. My value comes from what God said about me. My value comes from what God put inside me, which is a unique expression of His glory.

This may all sound a bit abstract and impersonal, so let me make it more personal.

Earlier, I said God is infinitely loving. God's love flows from His essential nature as a relational

Being.

God existed before time, perfectly content within Himself. However, it pleased Him to express His great love through His creation of human beings. He gave us the capacity to give and to receive love. This unique capacity was placed inside the human heart, or soul.

Other created beings also contain the capacity to give and receive affection, but no other created being rivals the depth and breadth of the human heart and soul to give and receive love. This is the unique glory given to human beings made as a reflection of God's essential nature. It is what God meant when He said, "Let us make man in our image."

So, our ability to love is a reflection of God's ability to love. However, God did not only make us lovers as a reflection of His essential nature as the original Lover. In addition to making us lovers in His own image, He also *loved* us.

> *We love because **he first loved us**.* (I John 4:19, emphasis added)

An essential element of authentic love is volition or will, reflecting the active desire of the lover to engage in a relationship with the beloved. God desires to give and receive authentic love. He placed in human beings the capacity to receive or reject His love for us.

Human Identity as Corrupted

Receiving God's love fully, giving Him all the credit and honor that is rightfully His as the Originator and Creator of all good things, and entering fully into a love relationship with Him is the highest and best human activity. It is how human beings reflect our essential nature with the greatest beauty. It is the only way to achieve self-actualization as human beings.

Rejecting God's love and choosing instead to ascribe greater value and worth to created things rather than to the Creator is the definition of evil.

The very first man and woman, Adam and Eve, lived in the perfect love relationship with God after He created them and placed them in the beautiful world that He made for them. They communicated with God and enjoyed His love. God promised them that He would continue to welcome them into His presence as long as they continued to prefer being with Him above all other choices. This preferring God to all other things is the definition of righteousness.

In order to demonstrate the contrast between the benefits of preferring God over created things (righteousness) and the cost of preferring created things over God (unrighteousness, also called "sin"), God created an alternative for Adam and

Eve and called it eating of the fruit on "the tree of the knowledge of good and evil":

> *And the Lord God commanded the man, saying, "You may surely eat of every tree of the garden, but of the tree of the knowledge of good and evil you shall not eat, for in the day that you eat of it you shall surely die."* (Genesis 2:16-17)

God promised that the cost of choosing this alternative would be the loss of their lives.

Adam and Eve chose the second option, because the fruit looked so good to them. They ate the fruit from the tree of the knowledge of good and evil, and evil came into the world.

The horrible cosmic effect of Adam's and Eve's choice was that evil permeated every element of creation, including every human being that was born after Adam and Eve.

Because of Adam's and Eve's choice, which we and all other human beings have also made, the following is now true:

> We have *exchanged the truth about God for a lie and worshiped and served the creature rather than the Creator, who is blessed forever!* (Romans 1:25)

> All creation groans in pain. *For we know that the whole creation has been groaning together in the pains of childbirth until now.* (Romans 8:22)

> Human beings are no longer able to choose or achieve ultimate goodness. We are no longer righteous. *None is righteous, no, not one; no one understands; no one seeks for God. All have turned aside; together they have become worthless; no one does good, not even one.* (Romans 3:10-12)

Every human being born after Adam and Eve has made the same choice that they did. We have lost our righteousness. We are no longer even able on our own to choose to receive God's love. There is part of us that is now dead, as God predicted. It is that part of us which wants to be with God and enjoy His love as we were intended to enjoy it.

Human Identity as Redeemable

God, being God, is essentially committed (and rightfully so) to upholding His transcendent beauty, or glory. As we have seen, His glory is the sum of all of his essential characteristics including His love, His power, His wisdom, His justice, and others.

Having created human beings with the capacity to either receive or reject His love, and human beings having rejected His love and having preferred created things over God Himself, God remained committed to upholding the beauty of His perfect justice. Justice requires that the cost of rejecting God's perfect love and settling for lesser things be fully borne or paid.

The essence of the death promised by God as the consequence of rejecting Him and eating of the tree of the knowledge of good and evil is eternal separation from God.

Separation is required because God's infinite perfection cannot stand to be polluted by the presence of sinful beings (including human beings) anymore than a beautiful bridal dress can stand to be polluted with human excrement and remain radiant or a pristine ocean can stand to be polluted by an oil spill and stay pure. These illustrations break down because bridal dresses and oceans, wonderful though they are, are created things and therefore can in fact be corrupted. God, the only Original being, cannot be corrupted. If He could, He would not be God.

Therefore, the result of Adam's and Eve's choice is that a great chasm has opened up between all created beings and things and God Himself. The existence of this chasm upholds God's justice, and if He had chosen to maintain this chasm forever, He would still be perfectly good, loving, just, wise, and powerful.

But He didn't choose that.

He chose instead to offer a new expression of love that is even greater than the love He expressed in making human beings and the rest of the created realm.

This new expression is greater than the original expression because it requires that God Himself put back into us His own essential goodness, or righteousness, in order to enable Him to receive us again into His presence without violating His own perfection and righteousness. It requires that He resurrect the part of us that died when we, with Adam and Eve, chose to prefer created things over the Creator. And it requires that God still uphold the glory of His perfect justice by finding a way for the full cost of human unrighteousness (sin) to be borne and paid.

This new expression is utterly loving because God chose to bear the cost and pay the price of human sin, my sin, Himself. He poured out the fully just consequences of human sin onto Himself so that human beings might again become righteous.

He accomplished this plan for the redemption of human beings by sending His Son, Jesus, Who is also fully God and equal in every way with His Father God, to give up His perfect power and infinite beauty that He shares with His Father and instead to take on all of the limitations and ugliness of being an imperfect human being (without actually committing sin Himself).

Not only did Jesus allow Himself to be reduced to being human, but He also allowed Himself to be rejected and murdered, undeservedly, in an excruciatingly painful and utterly shameful way.

Jesus and His Father agreed upon this plan, this superior expression of their love for human beings, in order to fully uphold the glory of God's justice and to magnificently express the glory of God's great love.

> *For our sake he made him to be sin who knew no sin,* ***so that in him we might become the righteousness of God.*** *(2 Corinthians 5:21, emphasis added)*

Through this divine exchange of my sin for the righteousness of God, the possibility of coming back into perfect relationship with God has been restored.

However, there is still a requirement that needs to be met in order for this possibility to be realized in my life.

The requirement is simple. I simply have to *receive* this love.

Receiving this love means accepting and declaring that I need it in order to be happy and whole, in order to be perfect and peaceful, in order to be satisfied and safe. It means acknowledging that I'm defective and deficient without it.

It means accepting that Jesus is the only answer and the complete answer to my desperate need.

It means looking outside myself to understand my identity and to achieve self-actualization.

What God Says About My Redeemed Identity

Listen to the wonderful voice of God in these Bible passages, declaring His Fatherly love for His redeemed people:

> *For you are a people holy to the Lord your God. The **Lord your God has chosen you to be a people for his treasured possession**, out of all the peoples who are on the face of the earth. **It was not because you were more in number than any other people that the Lord set his love on you and chose you**, for you were the fewest of all peoples, **but it is because the Lord loves** you and is keeping the oath that he swore to your fathers, that the Lord has brought you out with a mighty hand and redeemed you from the house of slavery, from the hand of Pharaoh king of Egypt.* (Deuteronomy 7:6-8, emphasis added)

These are words that God spoke to the people of Israel long before Jesus became a human and came into the world. God chose to have a unique love relationship with Israel that was a foretaste of God's intimate relationship with all humans that receive God's love offered through Jesus. In this passage, it is very clear that God's relationship with Israel was not offered on the basis of Israel's deserving or intrinsic value but rather on the basis of His own great love. The Bible teaches that all people that accept the offer of redemption given through Jesus are included in the promises given to Israel. So, if you are a follower of Jesus, this description of God's love refers not only to His love for Israel but also to His love for you.

Do you grasp the depth of this news? The God of the universe, Who is awesome in power and wisdom, has made a declaration of love about the people that receive His love. He has said, "I want you. You are beautiful to me. Not only am I going to take away your filth and shame caused by your sin, but I'm going to give you a new name and a new family (My family), a new inheritance, and a new future." This declaration is not about any value that is intrinsic to me, as this passage in Deuteronomy 7 makes very clear. It is only about what God has declared about me.

Getting past the shock of the "passiveness" of my role in my personal redemption can take time (after all, the desire to "prove" my value through my accomplishments goes very deep in my heart). It can feel like death. However, there comes a wonderful moment in the life of every follower of Jesus when the understanding of my own passivity in creating the essence of my identity brings a wellspring of delight and joy that no man-made identity can compare with. The reason it is so wonderful is that my God-given identity is permanent and secure. There is nothing I can do to mess it up! It is completely beyond my ability to change, tarnish, manipulate, lose, or improve. It simply is. The essence of my identity is what God says about me. Period.

Let me share some passages from the Bible to show the tenderness and warmth of God's love for His redeemed people:

> *The nations shall see your righteousness, and all the kings your glory, and you shall be called by a new name that the mouth of the Lord will give.* ***You shall be a crown of beauty in the hand of the Lord****, and a royal diadem in the hand of your God. You shall no more be termed Forsaken, and your land shall no more be termed Desolate, but **you shall be called My Delight Is in Her**, and your land Married; for **the Lord delights in you**, and your land shall be married. For as a young man marries a young woman, so shall your sons marry you, and as the bridegroom rejoices over the bride, **so shall your God rejoice over you.*** (Isaiah 62:2-5, emphasis added)

This passage heralds the reality that God delights in His people. His delight is in the righteousness and glory that He sees in us, which He has given to us. He has erased our desolation and forsakenness and replaced them with belonging and intimacy. Do you feel the love? You should feel it! It is real, it is personal, and it is directed at you. Savor it!

Here are two similar passages:

> *And when Jesus was baptized, immediately he went up from the water, and behold, the heavens were opened to him, and he saw the Spirit of God descending like a dove and coming to rest on him; and behold, **a voice from heaven said, "This is my beloved Son, with whom I am well pleased**."* (Matthew 3:16-17, emphasis added)

> *He was still speaking when, behold, a bright cloud overshadowed them, and **a voice from the cloud said, "This is my beloved Son, with whom I am well pleased; listen to him**."* (Matthew 17:5, emphasis added)

Both of these passages demonstrate the deep love of God the Father for His Son Jesus. I imagine Father God beaming with delight as He gazes on His radiant Son in all of His glory.

This fatherly love is not only for Jesus. It is also for followers of Jesus.

> *...in Christ Jesus you are all sons of God, through faith. For as many of you as were baptized into Christ have put on Christ. There is neither Jew nor Greek, there is neither slave nor free, there is no male and female, for you are all one in Christ Jesus. And if you are Christ's, then you are Abraham's offspring, heirs according to promise. I mean that the heir, as long as he is a child, is no different from a slave, though he is the owner of everything, but he is under guardians and man-*

> *agers until the date set by his father. In the same way we also, when we were children, were enslaved to the elementary principles of the world. But when the fullness of time had come, **God sent forth his Son**, born of woman, born under the law, to redeem those who were under the law, **so that we might receive adoption as sons. And because you are sons, God has sent the Spirit of his Son into our hearts, crying, "Abba! Father!" So you are no longer a slave, but a son, and if a son, then an heir through God.*** (Galatians 3:26-4:7, emphasis added)
>
> *For you did not receive the spirit of slavery to fall back into fear, but **you have received the Spirit of adoption as sons, by whom we cry, "Abba! Father!" The Spirit himself bears witness with our spirit that we are children of God, and if children, then heirs—heirs of God and fellow heirs with Christ**, provided we suffer with him in order that we may also be glorified with him.* (Romans 8:15-17, emphasis added)

These passages show wonderfully that the Father/Child relationship between God the Father and God the Son has been extended to followers of Jesus as well. United with Jesus and given His righteousness, we are also given sonship and daughtership. God is now our Father just as He is the Father of Jesus. The term "Abba" is a Hebrew term that means simply "father." The reason this term is used in these passages is that God's Fatherhood bestows rights and privileges on His offspring. It gives me a right to participate in a glorious inheritance as an heir (the inheritance of God's presence) and to have the power of my enemies (slavery to sin and fear) canceled and removed.

God has good things in store for His children.

> *...I will visit you, and I will fulfill to you my promise and bring you back to this place. For **I know the plans I have for you, declares the Lord, plans for welfare and not for evil, to give you a future and a hope**. Then you will call upon me and come and pray to me, and I will hear you. You will seek me and find me, when you seek me with all your heart. I will be found by you, declares the Lord, and **I will restore your fortunes** and gather you from all the nations and all the places where I have driven you, declares the Lord, and I will bring you back to the place from which I sent you into exile.* (Jeremiah 29:10-14, emphasis added)

This message was given by God to His children who were feeling forsaken and desolate. Echoing the promises God gave His children through Isaiah to give them a new name and family, this passage from Jeremiah answers similar questions about identity and purpose: Is there a purpose for me? Will my future be good? Will there be a place for me? Resoundingly, God answers "Yes!" for all those that seek Him with their whole heart. That is, for all that receive Him, He promises a good future.

Our rebirth from orphans to adopted sons and daughters of God brings with it a sure hope of an immeasurably great future.

> *Blessed be the God and Father of our Lord Jesus Christ! According to his great mercy,* **he has caused us to be born again to a living hope** *through the resurrection of Jesus Christ from the dead,* **to an inheritance that is imperishable, undefiled, and unfading, kept in heaven for you,** *who by God's power are being guarded through faith for a salvation ready to be revealed in the last time. In this you rejoice, though now for a little while, if necessary, you have been grieved by various trials, so that the tested genuineness of your faith—more precious than gold that perishes though it is tested by fire—may be found to result in praise and glory and honor at the revelation of Jesus Christ. Though you have not seen him, you love him. Though you do not now see him, you believe in him and rejoice with joy that is inexpressible and filled with glory, obtaining the outcome of your faith, the salvation of your souls.* (I Peter 1:3-9, emphasis added)

Peter's message was tailor-made for those that struggle with questions about identity, purpose, and future. Peter anticipates the question, "Is the inheritance I'm waiting on really there? Is it really good? It feels like the joy I once felt is fading like the recognition from winning a cross country race or from walking across the stage with honors at graduation. Those medals and diploma are collecting dust in a box somewhere, and the fleeting pleasure they produced has been long forgotten. Does that mean my inheritance is fading as well?" Resoundingly, Peter declares and assures, "No!" The inheritance is imperishable, undefiled, unfading, and kept in heaven! This hope is a sure and living hope! It is not a "maybe" hope, as in "maybe the sun will shine tomorrow." It is a sure and living hope. You can bet your life on this kind of hope.

This hope is in a future of position, authority, riches, life, and love, all given because of God's great love for us.

> *And you were dead in the trespasses and sins in which you once walked, following the course of this world, following the prince of the power of the air, the spirit that is now at work in the sons of disobedience— among whom we all once lived in the passions of our flesh, carrying out the desires of the body and the mind, and were by nature children of wrath, like the rest of mankind. But **God, being rich in mercy, because of the great love with which he loved us**, even when we were dead in our trespasses, **made us alive** together with Christ—by grace you have been saved—and **raised us up with him and seated us with him** in the heavenly places in Christ Jesus, **so that in the coming ages he might show the immeasurable riches of his grace in kindness toward us***

> *in Christ Jesus. For by grace you have been saved through faith. And this is not your own doing; it is the gift of God, not a result of works, so that no one may boast. For **we are his workmanship, created in Christ Jesus for good works, which God prepared beforehand, that we should walk in them.*** (Ephesians 2:1-10, emphasis added)

This passage shows the oppressive spirit ("prince of the power of the air") that used to rule over followers of Jesus, before they received God's righteousness. It shows what kind of children we were before we became God's children (sons of disobedience; children of wrath). It proclaims the great love of God that motivated Him to redeem and resurrect us. It shows that we have immeasurable riches waiting for us in heaven. It reminds us that our new identity is essentially a gift from God. Lastly, it shows that God has prepared good things for us to do. We will talk more about that in Parts Two and Three. For now, savor this incredibly good news. God has done this incredible work to transform my identity. What kindness! What great love! What a gift! What a God!

The Essence of My Identity and How I Feel About It

To summarize what we've covered, here is the essence of my identity as a follower of Jesus:

- Loved and chosen

- Adopted and fathered
- Planned and provided for
- Known and heard and seen
- Delighted in

At a very low point in my life in 2016, I felt the need for these realities more than I ever had before. Then, as I cried out to God, "I need You! Where are You? Help me! What is my purpose? Who am I? Do not leave me!" an amazing thing happened. I began to feel in the depth of my being the reality of God's fatherly, gentle, purposeful presence. I began to sense Him saying to me, "I am with you. I am smiling down on you. I see you. I hear you. I love you. You delight Me. I have really good things to show you, give you, and do through you. They won't just be good for Me. They will also be good for you. I will satisfy the deepest longings of your heart in a way that will astound you in its tenderness and comprehensiveness. You are Mine. I will never leave you." Then, almost as an afterthought, I sensed Him saying with a chuckle, "Just relax in Me."

This is the effect that grasping the essence of your identity as a follower of Jesus has on you. It causes the anxieties, doubts, fears, and a host of other negative feelings to fall away. Being emptied of fleeting man-made pseudo identities and being filled with the Spirit of Jesus has that effect on a person. This is what Paul had in mind in his wonderful prayer in his letter to the Ephesian church:

> *For this reason I bow my knees before the Father, from whom every family in heaven and on earth is named, that according to the riches of his glory* ***he may grant you to be strengthened with power through his Spirit in your inner being****, so that Christ may dwell in your hearts through faith—* ***that you****, being rooted and grounded in love,* ***may have strength to comprehend with all the saints what is the breadth and length and height and depth, and to know the love of Christ that surpasses knowledge, that you may be filled with all the fullness of God***. (Ephesians 3:14-19, emphasis added)

Follower of Jesus: For all of eternity, before space and time were created, you have existed in the mind of God as beloved (known, seen, heard, understood, chosen, loved, remembered, protected, treasured, established from before the foundation of the world).

I am praying right now for you to experience this same effect as you grasp the essence of your identity. Parts Two and Three will not be helpful to you if they are not built on this foundation of being a child of God, one with His Son Jesus.

Almighty Father and glorious Son, please apply these truths to the hearts of all who read this book by the power of Your Spirit, so that they may be ravished by Your great love and receive it in full.

Human Self-actualization: A Process of Reversal and Renewal

Human self-actualization is made possible only by following Jesus. By following Jesus, the effects of death in our lives are reversed, and we are renewed and restored back to God's original design for our unique expression of His glory.

This process is not always linear, from our perspective, though it is certainly linear from God's perspective. From our limited vantage point, it can feel like mountaintops and valleys, one step forward and three steps backward, life and death, seeing and blindness, hearing and deafness, wealth and poverty, beauty and shame, delight and bitterness, health and sickness.

This is how it is before the return of King Jesus to earth to take us to live with Him in heaven forever. The effects of our sin-polluted hearts are being reversed, but they are not yet eliminated. Sometimes the residual effects of sin remind us in ugly and painful ways that they are still there. Sometimes we still act like spiritual orphans instead of like the true heavenly princes and princesses that we are.

Over time, this seemingly absurd way of living makes more and more sense. Suffering is an element of transformation (see Romans 8:17) and does not last more than a little while (I Peter 5:10; 2

Corinthians 4:17). Death gives way to life (John 12:23-26). The imperfections in our character are pruned away by the all-wise Vinedresser (John 15:1-8). We are renewed in our inner man and woman (2 Corinthians 4:16) and changed from one degree of transcendent beauty to another (2 Corinthians 3:18).

Losing My Self, Finding My Identity

The key to victory in this difficult but infinitely worthwhile journey is to understand that we have to lose our identity in order to find it. We have to release our identity in order to regain it. We have to die in order to live.

Look at a few passages with me.

> *Truly, truly, I say to you, unless a grain of wheat falls into the earth and dies, it remains alone; but **if it dies, it bears much fruit**. Whoever loves his life loses it, and **whoever hates his life in this world will keep it for eternal life**.* (John 12:24-25, emphasis added)
>
> *I have been crucified with Christ. **It is no longer I who live, but Christ who lives in me**. And the life I now live in the flesh I live by faith in the Son of God, who loved me and gave himself for me.* (Galatians 2:20, emphasis added)
>
> *If then you have been raised with Christ, seek the things that are above, where Christ is, seated at*

the right hand of God. Set your minds on things that are above, not on things that are on earth. For **you have died, and your life is hidden with Christ in God. When Christ who is your life appears, then you also will appear with him** *in glory.* (Colossians 3:1-4, emphasis added)

Do you see the paradox here? Death is required in order to experience abundant life. Let all of your self-made identities die. Let all of your poses and self-defined images - the things you want others to see in you and believe about you -- let them all die. Submit your entire being (spirit, soul, body), including your desires, your emotions, your thoughts, your choices, your time, your possessions, your relationships, your *everything* to Jesus Christ so that you become hidden with Christ in God and He becomes your life. Then, you and others around you will begin to experience the real you that God had in mind before the foundation of the world. You will produce life-giving fruit for those around you to enjoy in ways that far exceed your own abilities and resources, because when you allow yourself to die, you enable others to experience the life of Jesus through your life.

Human Identity: From Essence to Expression

In my own story, after letting go of my self-made identity, submitting my future to Jesus, and simply basking in the beauty of the essence of my identity as a child loved by Father God, I still had an unanswered question for Him: "Now what?"

This question reflects the reality we saw in Ephesians 2 that God has planned good work for us to do. God wants us to express His transcendent beauty in our lives, just as a musical instrument expresses the beautiful melodies in the mind of the musician.

It is to this question that I will turn now, in two parts. In Part Two I will summarize three common expressions or roles that should be cultivated among all followers of Jesus. Then, in Part Three I will provide a framework that can help each follower of Jesus understand the unique expression of God's transcendent beauty that has been planned by God for him or her.

PART TWO: SHARED EXPRESSIONS OF IDENTITY AS FOLLOWERS OF JESUS

Your life is a short breath in the spectrum of eternity. You had a beginning, and one day you will die. The day of your death is coming as sure as you are living and breathing right now. There is a brief span of time called your life during which you have been given gifts of time, talents, and energy.

What is your purpose? What is the meaning of your life? Why are you here?

What did God have in mind when He made you?

What does He now want for you?

He wants to show something through you. He wants to offer something through you. What is it?

In Part One we saw that the essence of human identity is what God says about humans. The only way to maximize happiness as human beings is to receive our God-given identity as His children.

Having understood and received this new identity, followers of Jesus are left with the question "what now?"

As we saw in Part One, God made human beings as an expression of His transcendent beauty, or glory. He loves diverse expressions of glory! We see this in the magnificent display of cultures, landscapes, wildlife, smells, weather patterns, and people that exist in the world. God is a Master Artist Who expressed His glory breathtakingly when He made the earth, and He made human beings as the crown of His creation.

God did not make human beings to be immobile, basking motionlessly in our identity as children of God. He does want us to be at rest, and He does want us to bask. However, He also made us to act and to create, as reflections of His divine acting and creating. He has work for us to do! He has transformation for us to experience. His glory is revealed through us in a dynamic and progressive way that includes self-expression. It includes our energy and development; it includes utility and function. God didn't have to make the world this way. He could have made us all to be beautiful monuments or mirrors, stationary and picturesque. However, in His divine wisdom He made us alive.

The path to true self-actualization for each follower of Jesus is to seek to understand the expressions or roles of glory that God has planned for him or her. Some of these expressions are common to all followers of Jesus, and that is what we will examine in Part Two. In Part Three, we will examine how to answer the question, "Who am I uniquely and what did God make me uniquely to do?"

Before the return of King Jesus to reclaim His rightful place on the throne of the earth, the central role of followers of Jesus is to reflect His beauty in ways that sharply contrast with the brokenness, suffering, terrors, and horrors of the sin-corrupted world we live in.

There are three expressions or roles that all followers of Jesus are called to fill in our lives. These are roles that are inherently ours by virtue of our identity as followers of Jesus. Understanding these roles and learning how to practice them will lead to fruitfulness and gladness in our lives and communities. These roles are ambassador, sojourner, and warrior. Let's examine them together.

AMBASSADOR IDENTITY

The people of the world who do not know Jesus are dying. They are dying of thirst. They are dying of starvation. They are dying of isolation.

Follower of Jesus, you have a message for them that can quench their thirst, satisfy their hunger, and enable lasting relationships of love. This is good news!

Let's look at the ambassador identity together, understand how this identity was given to followers of Jesus, and imagine how we can express this identity in our living.

What Is an ambassador?

An ambassador is an essential role in any government that desires to promote peaceful relationships and co-existence with other nations.

There are three essential elements of an ambassador:

- The person or group being represented by the ambassador
- The message being delivered by the ambassador
- The people or group to whom the ambassador is going

Followers of Jesus as Ambassadors

The apostle Paul, one of the primary leaders of the first century Christian churches in southern Europe and the author of several letters in the Bible, saw himself as an ambassador. Look with me at the ways he used this language of "ambassador":

> *Therefore, if anyone is in Christ, he is a new creation. The old has passed away; behold, the new has come. All this is from God, who through Christ reconciled us to himself and gave us the ministry of reconciliation; that is, in Christ God was reconciling the world to himself, not counting their trespasses against them, and entrusting to us the message of reconciliation. Therefore,* **we are ambassadors for Christ, God making his appeal through us.** *We implore you on behalf of Christ, be reconciled to God. For our sake he made him to be sin who knew no sin, so that in him we*

> *might become the righteousness of God.* (2 Corinthians 5:17-21, emphasis added)

This wonderful passage contains the essence of the message (that unity with Jesus through the forgiveness of sin brings personal transformation and reconciliation with God), a reference to the One being represented by us as ambassadors (Christ), and a reference to the people to whom the message needs to be delivered (the world).

> *...praying at all times in the Spirit, with all prayer and supplication. To that end, keep alert with all perseverance, **making supplication** for all the saints, and also **for me, that words may be given to me in opening my mouth boldly to proclaim the mystery of the gospel, for which I am an ambassador in chains, that I may declare it boldly**, as I ought to speak.* (Ephesians 6:18-20, emphasis added)

This passage contains Paul's appeal for the prayers of the Ephesian church for Paul's ambassadorial ministry. Paul knew from experience that proclaiming the good news of hope offered through Jesus is not always easy or well-received. Therefore, boldness and clarity are needed, and it is essential to pray for these things.

> *"Therefore let it be known to you that **this salvation of God has been sent to the Gentiles; they will listen.**" He lived there two whole years at his own expense, and **welcomed all who came to him**,*

> ***proclaiming the kingdom of God and teaching about the Lord Jesus Christ with all boldness*** *and without hindrance.* (Acts 28:28-31, emphasis added)

In this passage at the end of the book of Acts, once again we see elements of the ambassadorial identity. The message (salvation of God; kingdom of God; the Lord Jesus Christ), the One being represented (God), and the people that God prepared to receive the message (Gentiles).

Paul was known as the "apostle to the Gentiles." Much of his ministry was conducted among Greek and Roman audiences that were non-Jewish but which were interested in ideas and power. Paul was very open to being directed and redirected by God. God's Spirit came to Paul multiple times in visions and told him where to stay or where to travel to. Sometimes the Spirit told him not to continue in a certain place. Other times, the Spirit told him to continue among a certain people group or region. At all times, Paul was a messenger, taking a message of hope and transformation to people who needed it and who were prepared by God to receive it, though not all received the message.

This ambassadorial identity was not original to Paul. It was commissioned by Jesus Himself. As He was leaving the earth to ascend into heaven after His resurrection, He made it clear that His followers were to take the message of hope offered through Jesus to the world. Look at three passages with me:

> *And Jesus came and said to them, "All authority in heaven and on earth has been given to me. **Go** therefore and **make disciples** of **all nations**, baptizing them in the name of the Father and of the Son and of the Holy Spirit, **teaching** them to observe **all that I have commanded you**. And behold, I am with you always, to the end of the age."* (Matthew 28:18-20, emphasis added)

> *Then he opened their minds to understand the Scriptures, and said to them, "Thus it is written, that the Christ should suffer and on the third day rise from the dead, and that **repentance for the forgiveness of sins** should be **proclaimed** in his name to **all nations**, beginning from Jerusalem.* (Luke 24:45-47, emphasis added)

> *But you will receive power when the Holy Spirit has come upon you, and you will be my **witnesses** in Jerusalem and in all Judea and Samaria, and to the **end of the earth**.* (Acts 1:8, emphasis added)

In these passages, we see all three elements of the ambassadorial identity. We see the One being represented (God, who has authority in heaven and on earth and has passed His authority and power to His disciples), the message ("all that I have commanded you" and "repentance for the forgiveness of sins"), and the groups to whom the message is to be taken ("all nations" and "the end of the earth").

Follower of Jesus: you have the message of hope that supersedes all other messages in its breadth and depth. It is the message human beings were made for. You are God's ambassador to the human beings in your life. Your family, your neighbors, your friends, your colleagues, your classmates, your teachers, your students, and your customers may never have another chance to hear the name of Jesus. Will you share Him with them?

Barriers to Being an Ambassador

It's sounds like a simple task, but in truth there are many barriers to being an ambassador for Jesus.

Here are some common barriers that I have observed:

- Overvaluing personal comfort and undervaluing relationships with people
- Lack of personal intimacy with God for the follower of Jesus (low desire to share Jesus with others since Jesus doesn't appear to mean much to the follower of Jesus himself)
- Cultural rejection of absolute truth (common in many contexts that have been influenced by Western culture)
- Fear of rejection by family members (common in many traditional cultures in which religion is an element of family identity)

- Perception of judgmental or condescending mindset among followers of Jesus (also common in many Western contexts)

There are many other barriers as well. What barriers have you experienced in your life as a follower of Jesus?

The answer to overcoming *all* barriers to being an ambassador is to be 100% convinced that the value of knowing Jesus is greater than all other values. It is the ultimate value. This is what Paul said made the difference in his own life:

> *But whatever gain I had, I counted as loss for the sake of Christ. Indeed,* ***I count everything as loss because of the surpassing worth of knowing Christ Jesus my Lord.*** *For his sake I have suffered the loss of all things and count them as rubbish, in order that I may gain Christ and be found in him....* (Philippians 3:7-9, emphasis added)

Paul made it his life mission to be an ambassador, no matter how much it cost him. He believed that the value of his message was greater than the value of anything else that he or anyone else could be preoccupied with.

Do you believe this?

Where to Start

If you see that the message of hope offered in

Jesus is necessary for all people and available to all people, here are some ways to express your ambassadorial identity:

- Pray. Ask God with an open and expectant heart to show you what to do and where to go. He will do more than you can imagine!
- Adopt a relational worldview. Begin to see the world as a sea of human hearts that were made for God and lost without Him. Every person you meet may be ready to receive Jesus.
- Seek opportunities to show unconditional love. Unconditional love is love offered with no expectation of receiving anything in return - no ulterior motive. Unconditional love sends a powerful message of value ("I value you") and can create unimaginable opportunities to engage spiritually with people.
- Make a list of the people in your life. Pray over the list, name by name, asking God to direct you to the people He has prepared in advance for you to engage with.
- Cultivate a glad and thankful demeanor. If you are not experiencing joy and gladness in your own life, others can perceive that. A negative spirit will not help communicate the love of Jesus effectively. Ask God and others to help you pinpoint the areas in your life that bring shame, anxiety, and bitterness so that you can experience healing and deliverance. Your own

joyful story of healing and deliverance will be compelling to those you engage with.
- Look for openings and opportunities. Everyone is a spiritual person, and everyone has deep desires that are part of being human. However, not everyone is conscious of spiritual things in any given moment or feeling the need to engage spiritually. Look for signs of anxiety, fear, bitterness, brokenness, pain, and isolation, and gently seek opportunities to ask probing questions that can lead to a discussion of hope.
- Trust God's leading. He will lead you. He will guide you. He is a thousand times more passionate about spreading His message of hope through you than you are. He is with you. He is working ahead of you. He has gone before you. He will give you every single thing you need.

SOJOURNER IDENTITY

Everyone longs for home. Deep in the heart of every human being is a desire for belonging, for security, for family, and for peace. The dream of home is an expression of these desires.

The Bible talks a lot about the concept of home. Our desires to belong, have security, have family, and have peace were placed in us by God. He intended us to search for these things, unsatisfied, until we find Him. Even after finding Him, the satisfaction of these desires is progressive, not reaching its climax until we are with God face to face in heaven.

Let's explore together the themes of home and the concept of sojourner discussed in the Bible, and then let's consider what this means for followers of Jesus.

What Is a Sojourner?

A sojourner is one who is a temporary resident in a place that is not his or her ultimate destination or home. If a diplomat or a soldier is stationed in a place for a certain amount of time with the intention of going back to a home country or region, he or she is a sojourner.

A sojourner is not necessarily a pilgrim or traveler. A sojourner can be stationary, living for a time in one place. The critical element to sojourning is the element of not being home in the fullest sense of "home." A sojourner is not fully at rest because he or she has not yet returned to the place he or she intends to find full belonging, security, family, and peace.

Let's look at some passages in the Bible about the concepts of sojourner and home. There are three elements of "home" that I see in the Bible:

1) God's people are not home yet. That is, we are sojourners.
2) God is the home of His people.
3) God's people are God's home.

While these are all of equal importance, I believe the first point is the most important one to emphasize for followers of Jesus in modern, wealthy societies because the predominant message we receive from the world is that this world as we know it is our home and that there is no better place that is still to come. That could not be further from the truth.

I want to quickly reiterate that all three of these are equally important, and you may need to be reminded of the second or third elements more urgently than you need the first. Let's explore together how the Bible talks about each of the three elements, and you can decide which message you need to lean most heavily on in your life presently.

Followers of Jesus Are Not Home Yet

The Bible teaches that, in one sense, followers of Jesus are not home yet. This world is not our final destination. We should see ourselves as foreigners in the world as we know it. Look at some passages with me.

> ***I am a sojourner on the earth****; hide not your commandments from me!* (Psalm 119:19, emphasis added)

> *But you are a chosen race, a royal priesthood, a holy nation, a people for his own possession, that you may proclaim the excellencies of him who called you out of darkness into his marvelous light. Once you were not a people, but now you are God's people; once you had not received mercy,*

*but now you have received mercy. Beloved, I urge you as **sojourners and exiles** to abstain from the passions of the flesh, which wage war against your soul. Keep your conduct among the Gentiles honorable, so that when they speak against you as evildoers, they may see your good deeds and glorify God on the day of visitation.* (I Peter 2:9-12, emphasis added)

*In my Father's house are many rooms. If it were not so, would I have told you that I go to prepare a place for you? And if **I go and prepare a place for you**, I will come again and will take you to myself, **that where I am you may be also**.* (John 14:2-3, spoken by Jesus, emphasis added)

*I have given them your word, and the world has hated them because **they are not of the world, just as I am not of the world**. I do not ask that you take them out of the world, but that you keep them from the evil one. **They are not of the world, just as I am not of the world**. Sanctify them in the truth; your word is truth. As you sent me into the world, so I have sent them into the world.* (John 17:14-18, spoken by Jesus, emphasis added)

*So then you are no longer strangers and aliens, but you are **fellow citizens with the saints and members of the household of God**, built on the foundation of the apostles and prophets, Christ Jesus himself being the cornerstone, in whom the whole structure, being joined together, grows into a holy*

> *temple in the Lord. In him you also are being built together into a dwelling place for God by the Spirit.* (Ephesians 2:19-22, emphasis added)
>
> *Brothers, join in imitating me, and keep your eyes on those who walk according to the example you have in us. For many, of whom I have often told you and now tell you even with tears, walk as enemies of the cross of Christ. Their end is destruction, their god is their belly, and they glory in their shame, with minds set on earthly things. But **our citizenship is in heaven**, and from it we await a Savior, the Lord Jesus Christ, who will transform our lowly body to be like his glorious body, by the power that enables him even to subject all things to himself.* (Philippians 3:17-21, emphasis added)

The message in these passages is clear that the world as we know it and perceive it presently is not our true home. The "world" or "earth" as it is used in these passages represents the evil kingdom of darkness over which our spiritual enemy Satan has been given limited and temporary authority. Followers of Jesus are being built into a different people and nation (I Peter 2 passage) and are now citizens of God's house rather than of the world (Ephesians 2 and Philippians 3 passages). In the expression of our sojourner identity, followers of Jesus offer a contrasting message that there is another place that is far better that is our true home. Therefore, we do not need to invest our time, talents, and energies in maximizing material experiences and possessions in order to experience "home." Our true home cannot be obtained or improved through earthly investments.

Consider your investments of time, energy, talents, and resources. Are you investing like a citizen of heaven or a citizen of this world? Where are you "banking" on your home being located? What home do you find yourself dreaming of? The retirement home in the mountains of Vermont or the beaches of Mexico, or the home in the presence of King Jesus? Heed the following words of King Jesus about maximizing your investments. You'll be richer for it!

> *Do not lay up for yourselves treasures on earth, where moth and rust destroy and where thieves break in and steal, but **lay up for yourselves treasures in heaven**, where neither moth nor rust destroys and where thieves do not break in and steal. For **where your treasure is, there your heart will be also**.* (Matthew 6:19-21, emphasis added)

Followers of Jesus Are at Home in God

While in one sense we are not home yet, in another very real sense, we are already home. The Bible teaches us, wonderfully, that God is our home. Because of the reconciling work of Jesus, we can now approach God in any moment through prayer and commune with Him in our hearts. This communion is real and wonderful. It is as real as lovers enjoying one another or a nursing mother cuddling her newborn when the baby is full and happy.

The word that best describes this experience of being at home in God is "abide." The apostle John uses this word in his account of Jesus' life (the Gospel of John) and in his first and second letters (I John and 2 John) in the Bible's New Testament. The passage with the most striking picture of the benefits of abiding in God and the costs of not abiding is in John 15. In this passage, Jesus uses the metaphor of a vineyard to describe the relationships among His followers, Himself, and His Father.

Followers of Jesus are fruit-bearing branches in the vineyard, attached to the life-giving vine which is Jesus Himself. We receive the essential life-giving sap of Jesus (His Spirit) flowing through us when we are grafted[3] into Him as one of His followers. The more we surrender to His Spirit and His word in us, the more fruit we bear. The Father of Jesus is the master vinedresser, walking lovingly among the branches with His pruning knife. He knows that we are imperfect branches. He loves us too much to leave our imperfections. He wants to maximize beautiful fruit. So, He cuts and prunes.

Every cut feels like death, but the aftermath of the pruning is more fruit and more love. This intimacy is unsurpassed by any other kind on the earth. It is simply rapturous. It is a taste of our heavenly home, and it is available to us now.

God is home for the follower of Jesus.

> *I am the true vine, and my Father is the vinedresser. Every branch in me that does not bear fruit he takes away, and every branch that does bear fruit he prunes, that it may bear more fruit. Already you are clean because of the word that I have spoken to you.* ***Abide in me****, and I in you. As the branch cannot bear fruit by itself, unless it abides in the vine, neither can you, unless you* ***abide in me****. I am the vine; you are the branches. Whoever abides in me and I in him, he it is that bears much fruit, for apart from me you can do nothing. If anyone does not abide in me he is thrown away like a branch and withers; and the branches are gathered, thrown into the fire, and burned. If you* ***abide in me****, and my words abide in you, ask whatever you wish, and it will be done for you. By this my Father is glorified, that you bear much fruit and so prove to be my disciples. As the Father has loved me, so have I loved you.* ***Abide in my love****. If you keep my commandments, you will* ***abide in my love****, just as I have kept my Father's commandments and abide in his love. These things I have spoken to you, that my*

> *joy may be in you, and that your joy may be full.* (John 15:1-11, emphasis added)

Jesus' language of abiding in God as our home is consistent with the language of the Psalms and Proverbs which show clearly that there is a sense of peace and security that is experienced by God's people when we trust in Him. Examine a few passages with me:

> ***He who dwells in the shelter of the Most High will abide in the shadow of the Almighty.*** *I will say to the Lord, "**My refuge and my fortress, my God,** in whom I trust." For he will deliver you from the snare of the fowler and from the deadly pestilence. He will cover you with his pinions, and **under his wings you will find refuge;** his faithfulness is a shield and buckler. You will not fear the terror of the night, nor the arrow that flies by day, nor the pestilence that stalks in darkness, nor the destruction that wastes at noonday. A thousand may fall at your side, ten thousand at your right hand, but it will not come near you. You will only look with your eyes and see the recompense of the wicked. Because **you have made the Lord your dwelling place—the Most High, who is my refuge**—no evil shall be allowed to befall you, no plague come near your tent.* (Psalm 91:1-10, emphasis added)

> *…whoever listens to me will **dwell secure** and will be at ease, without dread of disaster.* (Proverbs

1:33, emphasis added)

*The children of your servants shall **dwell secure**; their offspring shall be established before you.* (Psalm 102:28, emphasis added)

*God is our **refuge** and strength, a very present help in trouble.* (Psalm 46:1, emphasis added)

*In peace I will both lie down and sleep; for you alone, O Lord, make me **dwell in safety**.* (Psalm 4:8, emphasis added)

*It is better to **take refuge in the Lord** than to trust in man.* (Psalm 118:8, emphasis added)

*He alone is my rock and my salvation, **my fortress**; I shall not be greatly shaken.* (Psalm 62:2, emphasis added)

*The **Lord is a stronghold** for the oppressed, a **stronghold in times of trouble**.* (Psalm 9:9, emphasis added)

*So we have come to know and to believe the love that God has for us. God is love, and **whoever abides in love abides in God**, and God abides in him.* (I John 4:16, emphasis added)

Follower of Jesus: you are at home in God. Even now He can satisfy your deepest desires for home, security, and peace. When you feel disoriented, when you travel, when you move, when you experience homelessness, when you are an orphan, when you are alone: remember, God is your home. No matter where you are, you can lie down and sleep in peace, because He alone makes you dwell in safety.

Followers of Jesus Are God's Home

There is an even more glorious dynamic to this truth of God being our home. This dynamic is that He has come to be at home among us and within us.

Are you kidding me? God? At home in ME? This weak, self-centered, irritable, frustrating shell of a person? Why would He do that? HOW can He do that?

It is true. He loves you enough to make His home in you! Like you and me, He does not want to live in a dirty home. He wants to live in a clean and pure place. So, He is committed to purifying you and to abiding in you. Relish these passages with me:

> ***I will dwell among the people of Israel*** *and will be their God. And they shall know that I am the Lord their God, who brought them out of the land of Egypt **that I might dwell among them**. I am the Lord their God.* (Exodus 29:45-46, emphasis added)
>
> ***I will make my dwelling among you****, and my soul shall not abhor you. And **I will walk among you***

and will be your God, and you shall be my people. (Leviticus 26:11-12, emphasis added)

*...I heard one speaking to me out of the temple, and he said to me, "Son of man, this is the place of my throne and the place of the soles of my feet, where **I will dwell in the midst of the people of Israel forever**. And the house of Israel shall no more defile my holy name, neither they, nor their kings, by their whoring and by the dead bodies of their kings at their high places, by setting their threshold by my threshold and their doorposts beside my doorposts, with only a wall between me and them. They have defiled my holy name by their abominations that they have committed, so I have consumed them in my anger. Now let them put away their whoring and the dead bodies of their kings far from me, and **I will dwell in their midst forever**.* (Ezekiel 43:6-9, emphasis added)

*For thus says the One who is high and lifted up, who inhabits eternity, whose name is Holy: "**I dwell in the high and holy place, and also with him who is of a contrite and lowly spirit,** to revive the spirit of the lowly, and to revive the heart of the contrite.* (Isaiah 57:15, emphasis added)

*And many nations shall join themselves to the Lord in that day, and shall be my people. And **I will dwell in your midst**, and you shall know that the Lord of hosts has sent me to you.* (Zechariah 2:11, emphasis added)

> *And the **Word became flesh and dwelt among us**, and we have seen his glory, glory as of the only Son from the Father, full of grace and truth.* (John 1:14, emphasis added)
>
> *And I heard a loud voice from the throne saying, "Behold, **the dwelling place of God is with man. He will dwell with them**, and they will be his people, and God himself will be with them as their God.* (Revelation 21:3, emphasis added)

Follower of Jesus: When you feel alone, outcast, forsaken, or forgotten, remember: God is in you. God abides in you. God will finish the good work that He has started in you, and He will never leave you.

He is at home in you.

While We Wait

If you are like me, you may struggle hard against impatience. There are so many unfulfilled longings in my heart, and sometimes they make me want to scream.

Where are justice and equity?
Where are hope and joy?
Where are peace and safety?
Where are life and gladness?
Where are truth and clarity?
Where are purpose and meaning?

The ways in which these longings are still unsatisfied within us and within the world are pointers to the great reality of sojourning: We are not home yet.

As you wait, embrace the heart of a hopeful sojourner: home is coming soon!

As surely as the sun set last night and rose this morning, home is coming.

As surely as longing for love and suffering from pain have defined the life experiences of every human being, home is coming.

Keep your eyes on Jesus, who is your home. Abide with Him; walk with Him. He will deliver you safely to your final place of rest.

The words of Proverbs 4 are so helpful to remind me of the posture of a sojourner: looking straight ahead, yearning and waiting for home.

> ***Keep your heart*** *with all vigilance, for from it flow the springs of life. Put away from you crooked speech, and put devious talk far from you.* ***Let your eyes look directly forward, and your gaze be straight before you.*** *Ponder the path of your feet; then all your ways will be sure.* ***Do not swerve to the right or to the left****; turn your foot away from evil.* (Proverbs 4:23-27, emphasis added)

WARRIOR IDENTITY

Everyone knows that enemies are real. Enemies must be exposed, attacked, and destroyed. It is not sufficient to avoid enemies and simply criticize them on social media. True enemies must be confronted directly and powerfully.

Deep within each person is a warrior.

When the warrior within sees or experiences oppression, injustice, or inequity, the warrior is activated.

"No! Not on my watch! I will not stand by and let that injustice happen. I will fight. I will attack. I will set right the wrongs that others or I have experienced. Justice will prevail."

When someone cuts another person off in traffic, when someone cheats another person, or when someone deceives another person, the warrior is activated. When someone with power oppresses a person with weakness, the warrior is activated.

Consider this story, and consider whether the warrior within you is activated when you read it:

> *And the Lord sent Nathan to David. He came to him and said to him, "There were two men in a certain city, the one rich and the other poor. The rich man had very many flocks and herds, but the poor man had nothing but one little ewe lamb, which he had bought. And he brought it up, and it grew up with him and with his children. It used to eat of his morsel and drink from his cup and lie in his arms, and it was like a daughter to him. Now there came a traveler to the rich man, and he was unwilling to take one of his own flock or herd to prepare for the guest who had come to him, but he took the poor man's lamb and prepared it for the man who had come to him." Then David's anger was greatly kindled against the man, and he said to Nathan, "As the Lord lives, the man who has done this deserves to die, and he shall restore the lamb fourfold, because he did this thing, and because he had no pity."* (2 Samuel 12:1-6)

If you are a healthy human being, your inner warrior probably began screaming before you reached the end of this story. Your anger, like King David's, became kindled.

A good warrior is a fighter that is willing to endure great personal loss in order to personally promote justice and equity and to see evil overcome by good.

Followers of Jesus are warriors. The key questions we need to examine together, then, are the following:

1) What are we fighting for?
2) Who are the real enemies?
3) How do we fight?

Let's look at these questions together using the Bible to guide us.

1) What Are Followers of Jesus Fighting For?

A warrior, by definition, has a cause that he is fighting for. When there are no more causes, there will be no more warriors. There will only be memories of conquest.

What is the cause that followers of Jesus are fighting for?

The cause that followers of Jesus fight to the death for is the Kingdom of God.

What in the world is that?

Let's look at three questions to help us unpack the overarching question, "What are followers of Jesus fighting for?"

Here are three supporting questions:

a) What is the Kingdom of God?
b) What does the Kingdom of God look like?
c) Why does the Kingdom of God need to be fought for?

a) What is the Kingdom of God?

The Kingdom of God is the collection of connected domains in which He is the Supreme Ruler.

In one sense, God's Kingdom already extends to all domains of the universe, including all seen and unseen realms (spiritual, physical, etc.). God made it all to reflect His transcendent beauty, and He sits above it all, the One Sovereign King ruling with supreme power and perfect justice. The Bible teaches this clearly:

> *The Lord has established his throne in the heavens, and his kingdom rules over all.* (Psalm 103:19)

> *Your kingdom is an everlasting kingdom, and your dominion endures throughout all generations. [The Lord is faithful in all his words and kind in all his works.] The Lord upholds all who are falling and raises up all who are bowed down. The eyes of all look to you, and you give them their food in due season. You open your hand; you satisfy the desire of every living thing. The Lord is righteous in all his ways and kind in all his works.* (Psalm 145:13-17)

In another sense, which is probably much easier for many of us to understand than the first sense because it fits with our daily experience of living, God's Kingdom has not yet fully extended to all domains. Suffering and pain persist in the parts of the universe (including our own bodies) in which God's Kingdom has not yet fully been realized.

b) What Does the Kingdom of God Look Like?

The Kingdom of God looks like everything good that can be imagined, and more. It is the place where all of the deep desires of every human being for belonging, peace, security, transcendence, beauty, impact, understanding, and intimacy, are fully satisfied.

It is like the best dream you ever had.

Here is how it is described in the Bible:

> *Then I saw a new heaven and a new earth, for the first heaven and the first earth had passed away, and the sea was no more. And I saw the holy city, new Jerusalem, coming down out of heaven from God, prepared as a bride adorned for her husband. And I heard a loud voice from the throne saying, "Behold, the dwelling place of God is with man. He will dwell with them, and they will be his people, and God himself will be with them as their God. He will wipe away every tear from their eyes, and death shall be no more, neither shall there be mourning, nor crying, nor pain anymore,*

for the former things have passed away." And he who was seated on the throne said, "Behold, I am making all things new." Also he said, "Write this down, for these words are trustworthy and true." And he said to me, "It is done! I am the Alpha and the Omega, the beginning and the end. To the thirsty I will give from the spring of the water of life without payment. The one who conquers will have this heritage, and I will be his God and he will be my son. But as for the cowardly, the faithless, the detestable, as for murderers, the sexually immoral, sorcerers, idolaters, and all liars, their portion will be in the lake that burns with fire and sulfur, which is the second death." (Revelation 21:1-8)

And I saw no temple in the city, for its temple is the Lord God the Almighty and the Lamb. And the city has no need of sun or moon to shine on it, for the glory of God gives it light, and its lamp is the Lamb. By its light will the nations walk, and the kings of the earth will bring their glory into it, and its gates will never be shut by day—and there will be no night there. They will bring into it the glory and the honor of the nations. But nothing unclean will ever enter it, nor anyone who does what is detestable or false, but only those who are written in the Lamb's book of life. (Revelation 21:22-27)

These words bring tears to my eyes. Imagining a real place where I will live forever, where my thirst will continuously be quenched perfectly and my desires will continuously be met is an unbelievably great vision. It is what I want more than anything in the world.

c) Why Does It Need to Be Fought For?

The Kingdom of God needs to be fought for because it is under attack.

This might sound strange since we just established that, in a sense, the Kingdom extends to all realms (see Psalm 103 and Psalm 145 excerpts above) and that God is the Supreme Ruler over all.

While that is completely true, in God's wisdom He has allowed inferior challengers to come into existence in order that God's supremacy and superiority might be demonstrated by the contrast between His goodness and their ugliness and also by their eventual defeat and removal from the world. It is those inferior challengers that are the enemies of God's Kingdom.

Incredibly, God has planned that His followers (you and me) be part of His plan to fight and defeat the challengers of His authority and participate in the establishment of His eternal reign once and for all.

So, we have seen that followers of Jesus are fighting for the Kingdom of God, the place where He reigns supreme. His Kingdom is perfect and wonderful, but it is also under attack.

2) Who Are the Real Enemies of Followers of Jesus?

So who are these challengers that dare to seek to dethrone King Jesus and destabilize His wonderful Kingdom?

They are an insidious pair that work in the shadows, using deception and fear to gain control over people and manipulate them. The result of their work is destruction, isolation, and death.

Part of what makes this pair so powerful is that they seek to remain hidden and undetected. They seek to exploit the warrior within each human being and to pit human beings against one another, resulting in great destruction.

It is not good for this pair of challengers to remain unknown. Let us name them together.

The true enemies of the Kingdom of God and of followers of Jesus are sin and Satan.

They are a force (sin) and a person (Satan) that work together to wage war on followers of Jesus and His Kingdom. Let us examine this pair.

<u>What Is Sin?</u>

Sin is a disease that entered the world the moment that the first person chose to prefer something over God Himself. It is a corruption that dehumanizes and destabilizes human desire, emotion, thought, and will.

Human beings were made for God. As we saw in Part One, the essence of human identity is what God says about us. The more deeply human beings accept what God says with a posture of humility and trust, the more fully they will experience life and joy and peace.

Sin seeks to destabilize human identity by sending a mixture of new messages, all designed to deceive and take advantage of our natural desires:

- God is not loving or good
- God is not trustworthy
- God is not all-powerful
- God is not real

Sin is the inclination to direct my body, soul, and spirit to do something for which the ultimate outcome is anything other than making God look great. By taking advantage of human weakness and desire, sin seeks to produce death by making false things seem true and bad things seem good.

Followers of Jesus have been delivered from slavery to sin through the sin-conquering death and resurrection of Jesus. This means that followers of Jesus now have the power to say no to sin and yes to Jesus, every day. We now have the power to be delivered from the ways sin has corrupted us and stolen good things from us. The effects of sin in our lives can be redeemed and reversed. We can experience renewal and healing.

However, the smell of sin still lingers in the life of followers of Jesus, and the gangrenous power of sin still seeks to gain influence over us. It still threatens to undermine our relationships, our choices, and our well-being.

This passage from Romans 7 effectively describes the war being waged by sin for the heart of followers of Jesus:

> *Did that which is good, then, bring death to me? By no means!* ***It was sin, producing death in me through what is good, in order that sin might be shown to be sin****, and through the commandment might become sinful beyond measure. For we know that the law is spiritual, but I am of the flesh, sold under sin. For I do not understand my own actions. For I do not do what I want, but I do the very thing I hate. Now if I do what I do not want, I agree with the law, that it is good. So now **it is no longer I who do it, but sin that dwells within me**. For I know that nothing good dwells in me, that is, in my flesh. For I have the desire to do what is right, but not the ability to carry it out. For I do not do the good I want, but the evil I do not want is what I keep on doing. Now if I do what I do not want, **it is no longer I who do it, but sin that dwells within me**. So I find it to be a law that **when I want to do right, evil lies close at hand**. For I de-*

> *light in the law of God, in my inner being, but I see in my members another law waging war against the law of my mind and making me captive to the law of sin that dwells in my members. Wretched man that I am! Who will deliver me from this body of death? Thanks be to God through Jesus Christ our Lord! So then, I myself serve the law of God with my mind, but with my flesh I serve the law of sin.* (Romans 7:13-25, emphasis added)

Follower of Jesus, beware of the deceptive traces of sin in your life. Root them out ruthlessly, and you will experience joy and peace in your life and with others.

Who Is Satan?

While sin is an impersonal force, Satan is a spiritual angel that was created by God to be beautiful and powerful. Satan's evolution into an agent of evil happened when he became self-absorbed rather than God-absorbed. As we saw above, being self-absorbed is the definition of sin.

God's commitment to upholding and proclaiming the supremacy of His own value above all other values is His righteousness, as we saw in Part I. When someone or something challenges God's supreme value, God is rightfully obligated to remove it from His presence and His Kingdom. So, God banished Satan from heaven in dramatic fashion. The account, described from God's perspective, of Satan's fall from glory and emergence as an enemy of God is found in Ezekiel chapter 28:

> *You were the signet of perfection, full of wisdom and perfect in beauty. You were in Eden, the garden of God; every precious stone was your covering, sardius, topaz, and diamond, beryl, onyx, and jasper, sapphire, emerald, and carbuncle; and crafted in gold were your settings and your engravings. On the day that you were created they were prepared. You were an anointed guardian cherub. I placed you; you were on the holy mountain of God; in the midst of the stones of fire you walked. You were blameless in your ways from the day you were created, till unrighteousness was found in you. In the abundance of your trade you were filled with violence in your midst, and you sinned; so I cast you as a profane thing from the mountain of God, and I destroyed you, O guardian cherub, from the midst of the stones of fire. Your heart was proud because of your beauty; you corrupted your wisdom for the sake of your splendor. I cast you to the ground; I exposed you before kings, to feast their eyes on you. By the multitude of your iniquities, in the unrighteousness of your trade you profaned your sanctuaries; so I brought fire out from your midst; it consumed you, and I turned you to ashes on the earth in the sight of all who saw you. All who know you among the peoples are appalled at you; you have come to a dreadful end and shall be no more forever.* (Ezekiel 28:12-19)

Jesus Himself witnessed Satan's dramatic fall from glory, as He testified in Luke's account:

> *And he said to them, "I saw Satan fall like lightning from heaven. Behold, I have given you authority to tread on serpents and scorpions, and over all the power of the enemy, and nothing shall hurt you.* (Luke 10:18-19, spoken by Jesus to His followers)

For a limited time and in limited domains, God has given Satan limited authority to build a kingdom for himself. Seething with anger over his fall from glory and hating the God who will not allow His glory to be shared with another, Satan's aim is to take down with himself as many other victims as he can. He seeks to steal, kill, and destroy by making sin look appealing to human beings.

Satan's methods are cunning and diverse, but fear and deception are never far away. He understands human desire and psychology very deeply, and he seeks to play mind games of manipulation. We will explore in the next section how to overcome these deceptive methods, but first let us examine some examples of his methods from the Bible.

> *Now the **serpent was more crafty than any other beast of the field** that the Lord God had made. He said to the woman, "Did God actually say, 'You shall not eat of any tree in the garden'?" And the woman said to the serpent, "We may eat of the*

fruit of the trees in the garden, but God said, 'You shall not eat of the fruit of the tree that is in the midst of the garden, neither shall you touch it, lest you die.'" But the serpent said to the woman, "You will not surely die. For God knows that when you eat of it your eyes will be opened, and you will be like God, knowing good and evil." So when the woman saw that the tree was good for food, and that it was a delight to the eyes, and that the tree was to be desired to make one wise, she took of its fruit and ate, and she also gave some to her husband who was with her, and he ate. Then the eyes of both were opened, and they knew that they were naked. And they sewed fig leaves together and made themselves loincloths. (Genesis 3:1-7, emphasis added)

Several of Satan's calling cards are evident in this passage. First, notice that Satan skillfully used the a partial truth to weave a deceptive narrative about God. He said (through a question), "God did not say you can't eat of any tree in the garden." This is true, God did not say that. However, Satan's intent was to cast doubt on the actual commandment of God, which was that Adam and Eve may not eat of the tree of the knowledge of good and evil. After casting doubt on God's good character and intention to bless Adam and Eve, Satan appealed to Eve's desire for good things (knowledge and wisdom, good food, and beautiful things to look at). In doing this, Satan successfully lured Adam and Eve away from God Himself, and they sinned. There is also fear in this story. Satan tempted Adam and Eve to fear the absence of God's blessing.

Several other passages in the Bible demonstrate Satan's methods. It is so important to learn Satan's ways so that we can learn to fight him with dexterity and skill. For further study, here are several more passages:

- Zechariah 3:1-5 (Satan seeks to accuse Joshua of unworthiness.)

- Job 1:6-12; 2:1-10 (Satan causes a man named Job to suffer so that he will despair and turn away from God.)

- Matthew 4:1-11 (Satan tempts Jesus to worship him instead of worshiping God in order to have grounds to accuse Jesus.)

- I Peter 5:8-10 (Peter reminds followers of Jesus that Satan is always on the prowl, seeking to hurt us.)

- Revelation 12:7-12; 13:1-10; 20:1-3; 20:7-10 (Satan is in a cosmic war against God, seeking to accuse and deceive human beings.)

Follower of Jesus, do you see the fruit of Satan's work? He aims to steal (life, joy, peace, confidence), to kill, and to destroy.

He works in the shadows and in the darkness, attempting to avoid being perceived or identified. However, his Achilles heel is his calling card.

He always leaves behind a web of isolation, destruction, bondage, violence, pain, and division. Where you see these things, you can be sure that Satan is close at hand, angling for leverage, exulting defiantly in the cheap victories he extracts for himself, and gloating over the carnage he is leaving.

But Satan's victories will be short-lived. Followers of Jesus carry with them weapons that Satan has no chance of stopping. No weapon formed against followers of Jesus succeed if we fight victoriously.

3) How Do Followers of Jesus Fight Victoriously?

So, then, let us examine how to fight victoriously!

Followers of Jesus fight victoriously against sin and Satan by the following:

a) Placing our faith in God as revealed in His word

b) Waiting on Him and surrendering to Him in prayer

c) Wielding the weapons He gives us in the

spiritual battles we encounter

Let's examine these individually.

a) Faith in Jesus as Revealed in His Word

The first step for the follower of Jesus in every challenge is to believe in God's power and goodness. Look at the passages above about how Satan works. He seeks to sow seeds of unbelief that disrupt the connection between Jesus and His followers. Faith puts the spotlight back on God and opens the door for Him to powerfully rescue His followers. Jesus declared God's sufficiency and His unique right to receive worship when He was tempted by Satan. He strengthened His own faith by quoting and depending on promises in God's word. Also, in I Peter 5:8-10, Peter exhorted steadfast faith in God as the first foundation for resisting Satan's influence.

Follower of Jesus: read the Bible. Memorize it. Devour it more eagerly than food. Get its promises deep inside your heart and mind. They will be a lifeline for you in your moments of battle, and they will enable you to strengthen others as well. Think God's thoughts after Him, feel His feelings, and understand His heart. Remember what He says about you and the essence of your identity. Remember His heart of love toward you.

The deeper you go into God's heart as He is revealed in the Bible, the deeper the roots of your faith will go in your heart and the more steadfast you will be in your fight against sin and Satan.

b) Waiting on and Surrendering to Jesus in Prayer

Prayer and waiting on God are two sides of the same coin of total surrender. We saw in Revelation 12:11 above that the saints who surrendered their very lives to God were able to conquer Satan. Prayer acknowledges God as the source of all power and authority. The concept of "waiting" is a wonderful picture of God as the primary mover, leader, and guide of all circumstances in our lives. The Bible is full of promises of deliverance for those who wait on God and hope in His sure deliverance.

Jesus Himself understood this and routinely withdrew from the people He ministered to in order to be alone with God in prayer, recognizing the importance of activating His ministry through a posture of surrender to God.

Follower of Jesus: get alone with God. Share your heart with Him. Listen to Him. Ask Him where He is leading you, and go there with Him. Do not act until He gives you peace and confidence.

This process of listening to God in prayer often brings to mind sin patterns to be repented of. Repent quickly and eagerly. Repentance brings clarity. With repentance, you will hear God's voice more clearly in your heart. You will see the battlegrounds in your life with greater perception and discernment, and you will be able to wield your weapons of warfare with greater skill and dexterity.

c) Wielding the Weapons of Jesus in Our Battles

What are these spiritual weapons that we have been given? The best place to find a clear list of the weapons is in Paul's letter to the Ephesian church.

> *Finally, be strong in the Lord and in the strength of his might. Put on the whole armor of God, that you may be able to stand against the schemes of the devil. For we do not wrestle against flesh and blood, but against the rulers, against the authorities, against the cosmic powers over this present darkness, against the spiritual forces of evil in the heavenly places. Therefore take up the whole armor of God, that you may be able to withstand in the evil day, and having done all, to stand firm. Stand therefore, having fastened on the belt of truth, and having put on the breastplate of righteousness, and, as shoes for your feet, having put on the readiness given by the gospel of peace. In all circumstances take up the shield of faith, with which you can extinguish all the flaming darts of the evil one; and take the helmet of salvation, and the sword of the Spirit, which is the word of God, praying at all times in the Spirit, with all prayer and supplication. To that end, keep alert with all perseverance, making supplication for all the*

saints.... (Ephesians 6:10-18)

We see in this passage that God's power is the fuel for our fighting ("Be strong in the Lord and in the strength of His might.") and that He has given us spiritual armor for victorious fighting. Here are a few words about each of the weapons, along with other helpful Bible passages that help to unpack the meaning of the weapons:

- Truth - We must always prioritize at the forefront of our minds and hearts the truth about God's power and goodness revealed in His word. This will help us fight against the deceptive influences of sin and Satan.
- Righteousness - We must prioritize God with every fiber of our being, putting Him above all other aims and goals. This is the definition of righteousness.
- Readiness - We must always be prepared, like a good soldier, to move and to fight. Do not be lethargic or listless.
- Peace - We must remember that **human beings are not our enemies**, though they often *feel* like our enemies. We bring a message of reconciliation and peace. This is the Gospel.
- Faith - We must place our faith in God alone. This causes the attacks from the enemy to be extinguished by our shield of faith before they can penetrate our hearts.
- Salvation identity - We must savor our salvation identity, which sits on our heads ("hel-

met of salvation") and is meant to protect us from lies about our identity. We are saved and loved, redeemed and adopted.

- Word of God - We must keep God's Word always with us in our heart and mind, ready to counter the lies that we and others are tempted to believe. God's Word, which is the truth about Him that has been spoken by His messengers and recorded in the Bible, pierces the darkness of confusion and deceit, bringing life and fullness.

For the word of God is living and active, sharper than any two-edged sword, piercing to the division of soul and of spirit, of joints and of marrow, and discerning the thoughts and intentions of the heart. (Hebrews 4:12)

- Spirit-led prayer - We must pray without ceasing. The Spirit of God intercedes for us and leads us to pray God's will in all circumstances (need, longing, fear, temptation, rejoicing, etc.). Listen to the Spirit. Follow the Spirit's leading. Join the Spirit in seeking God's heart for your choices, your desires, and your obedience. He will show you.

Likewise the Spirit helps us in our weakness. For we do not know what to pray for as we ought, but the Spirit himself intercedes for us with groanings too deep for words. And he who searches hearts knows what is the mind of the Spirit, be-

cause the Spirit intercedes for the saints according to the will of God. (Romans 8:26-27)

- Alertness - We must be watchful. Satan is not easy to perceive, but he is also not invisible. We will notice his presence if we are looking for it.
- Perseverance - We must not give up or grow weary. We will reap a good reward if we persevere!

And let us not grow weary of doing good, for in due season we will reap, if we do not give up. (Galatians 6:9)

Follower of Jesus: you have been given abundant weapons to wield against your enemies. If you wield them with diligence and humility, you can expect an abundant harvest of blessing in this life and in the life to come. You will experience joy and peace, and you will bring life and peace to many others.

Conclusion

One final word of motivation for followers of Jesus: an immeasurably glorious reward awaits the victorious follower of Jesus.

The one who conquers, I will grant him to sit with me on my throne, as I also conquered and sat down with my Father on his throne. (Revelation 3:21)

So, follower of Jesus: you are an ambassador, a sojourner, and a warrior. These expressions of your identity as a child of God are common to all followers of Jesus. Let us examine next how to discover the unique expressions of identity that only you were made to express.

PART THREE: YOUR UNIQUE EXPRESSIONS OF IDENTITY AS A FOLLOWER OF JESUS

In Part One we examined the foundation of the sense of self for followers of Jesus, which is that we have been declared to be beloved children of God. This is the essence of our identity to which we must continually return when we feel that our identity is threatened or undermined.

In Part Two we examined expressions of the identity of followers of Jesus which are common among all of His followers. Each of these (ambassador, sojourner, and warrior) is temporary and will find its fulfillment and its end when we are, at last, face to face with Jesus.

An ambassador is not needed when the King is present.
A sojourner is no longer sojourning when he has reached his final resting place.
A warrior can lay down his weapons for the last time once the war is won.

In Part Three we will examine the unique expression of identity that each follower of Jesus has been designed to express.

God is a creative genius. As we saw in Part One, He loves to display His infinite beauty through a tapestry of unique expressions in the universe. Just as each human being contains a unique set of physical genes which manifest God's never-seen-before and nothing-quite-like-it beauty in that person's physical appearance and personality, so also does each human being contain the capacity to uniquely reveal the beauty of God's spiritual character in his or her own life in a new way.

Paradoxically, the truth revealed in each expression of human identity, which is a particular and unique element of God's immeasurable transcendent beauty in that person, is not new. The truth has always existed in the mind of God from all eternity. The truth itself is unchanging. What is new is the specific expression of the truth in the life of each person.

My aim in Part Three is to equip you as a follower

of Jesus to understand the unique expression of your identity for which God has made you and to help you learn to express it with confidence.

EXPRESSION VS. ESSENCE

Before diving in to understanding your unique expression of God's glory, I have a cautionary word.

Never, ever, ever confuse the *expression* of your identity with the *essence* of your identity. If you remember anything at all from this book, remember this!

One of Satan's oldest tricks, with which he has successfully tricked billions of people into eternal slavery, is to deceive people into believing that they *are* what they *do*. That is a lie.

I am who God says I am. Jesus loves me. That is who I am. That is my name. That is my safe place. That is my strong tower. That is my refuge. That is my family. That is my birthright. That is my treasure. That is all I need. That is everything.

Who Am I?

In your dark moments,
when you feel alone and isolated,
when the prospect of failure enters your mind with ominous foreboding, threatening to undermine your reputation and power,
when you feel unnoticed and unheard,
when you feel you don't know what you should do,
when what you have done is not received or recognized....

Remember who you are. You are a child of the King. You are beloved. You are known. You are delighted in.

Each night before my youngest daughter goes to sleep, I speak these words over her:

"Daddy loves you. You are Daddy's girl.
Mommy loves you. You are Mommy's girl.
Jesus loves you. You are Jesus' girl.
Jesus will always be with you.
Jesus will always take care of you."

These things are her essence. They are yours too, if you are a Jesus-follower.

God has indeed made you to *do* things. He has prepared *work* for you to do.

The doing *expresses* your identity and manifests God's glory in you but does not *create* God's glory in you. This is the same as a musician playing different complementary instruments. Music emanates from a flute, a trumpet, and a trombone in uniquely beautiful ways, all from the mouth of the same musician. The music does not create the beauty of the instrument. The music simply reveals the unique beauty in the mind of the musician that he desired to demonstrate through that instrument.

God is...

- ...the Inventor: God created the musical instruments; He is the Potter and we are the clay He has made.

   *But now, O Lord, **you are our Father;** we are the clay, and **you are our potter;** we are all the work of your hand.* (Isaiah 64:8, emphasis added)

- ...the Composer: God wrote the music we are to express; He prepared work for us to do.

   *For we are his workmanship, created in Christ Jesus for **good works, which God prepared beforehand**, that we should walk in them.* (Ephesians 2:10, emphasis added)

- ...the Instrumentalist: God is the Musician blowing into His instruments the power and musical expression in His mind; His Spirit in us moves us to action and expression of His glory.

> *But if Christ is in you, although the body is dead because of sin, **the Spirit is life** because of righteousness. If the Spirit of him who raised Jesus from the dead dwells in you, **he who raised Christ Jesus from the dead will also give life to your mortal bodies through his Spirit who dwells in you**.* (Romans 8:10-11, emphasis added)

Followers of Jesus: you are the instruments! While we have each been made for unique expressions in God's master symphony, our identity comes not from the sound we make but rather from the God-given identity stamped on the bottom of each of our hearts: bona fide child of God.

THE DEPOSIT IN YOU

Timothy was a young pastor in the early first century church. He was one of the church leaders whose development the apostle Paul invested heavily in. Helped by Paul's fatherly investment in his life, Timothy developed into a dynamic and well-respected leader in the Ephesian church.

Paul's love for Timothy is very clearly demonstrated in several New Testament letters. There is no mistaking Paul's sincere affection for Timothy and the intimacy they enjoyed. For example, savor these opening verses of Paul's second letter to Timothy, and feel Paul's affectionate heart toward Timothy:

> *To Timothy,* ***my beloved child****: Grace, mercy, and peace from God the Father and Christ Jesus our*

Lord. I thank God whom I serve, as did my ancestors, with a clear conscience, as I remember you constantly in my prayers night and day. **As I remember your tears, I long to see you, that I may be filled with joy.** *I am reminded of your sincere faith, a faith that dwelt first in your grandmother Lois and your mother Eunice and now, I am sure, dwells in you as well.* (2 Timothy 1:2-5, emphasis added)

What love! This brings tears to my eyes, and it brings to my mind tender words that father figures in my own life have spoken to me.

Paul's intention in writing his letters to Timothy was to build Timothy up in his work as a young pastor, giving him guidance and instruction for how to do his work.

An element of this guidance was to remind Timothy of who he was (essence) and to remind him of how to act and function (expression).

One of the most striking exhortations that Paul gives to Timothy appears in both of Paul's letters to Timothy:

O Timothy, **guard the deposit entrusted to you***....* (1 Timothy 6:20, emphasis added)

By the Holy Spirit who dwells within us, **guard the good deposit entrusted to you***.* (2 Timothy 1:14, emphasis added)

While Paul had something specific in mind for Timothy in particular, referring to Timothy's anointing as a pastor and preacher in the Ephesian church, this statement paints a helpful picture of the reality that I would like to describe in Part Three: God has a unique expression in mind that He intends for each follower of Jesus to offer of His transcendent beauty.

These verses contain four elements that I would like to unpack: "Guard," "deposit," "entrusted," and "you."

Guard

This word implies that something about the deposit is under threat. Does this sound familiar? We saw in Part Two that Satan seeks to steal from, kill, and destroy followers of Jesus. More than anything, he wants to prevent us from expressing our essence as followers of Jesus and children of God.

Be alert! Be watchful! Use your weapons to engage the warrior in you! Be on your guard against thieves who want to keep you from displaying God's beauty as you were uniquely designed to do.

Remember who you are.

Deposit

This word implies something of value that has

been placed in you which God intends others to benefit from. For Timothy, the deposit was his pastoral ministry of shepherding and preaching to the people of God at Ephesus.

God has something in mind for you too. There is a deposit in you that God intends others to benefit from when it is on display in you, like a beautiful painting deposited inside a secure display case in an art gallery. The secure display case does not keep others from benefiting from the painting; it is not a barrier. Rather, it enables the painting to be guarded so that it can be enjoyed by many people. The painting has a dynamic role to play of creating joy and delight in the hearts of its observers.

So it is with the deposit in you.

Entrusted

This word implies safekeeping by a manager. A steward is someone who cares for something of value that is owned by someone else. Stewardship involves a relationship of trust between the owner and the steward. The owner has entrusted something of value to the steward, trusting that the steward will increase the value and the use of the thing of value during the duration of his stewardship. The steward trusts that he will be rewarded by the owner for his good work.

God is the supreme owner of everything. Everything good about you: your intelligence, your material possessions, your relationships, your education, your physical abilities, all of these things have been entrusted to you by God.

> *For from him and through him and to him are all things. To him be glory forever. Amen.* (Romans 11:36)

You

You are an individual. God made you individually and uniquely. He made you for an individual and unique purpose. You matter. God sees you. God knows you.

> *O Lord, you have searched me and known me! You know when I sit down and when I rise up; you discern my thoughts from afar. You search out my path and my lying down and are acquainted with all my ways. Even before a word is on my tongue, behold, O Lord, you know it altogether. You hem me in, behind and before, and lay your hand upon me. Such knowledge is too wonderful for me; it is high; I cannot attain it.... For you formed my inward parts; you knitted me together in my mother's womb. I praise you, for I am fearfully and wonderfully made. Wonderful are your works; my soul knows it very well. My frame was not hidden from you, when I was being made*

in secret, intricately woven in the depths of the earth. Your eyes saw my unformed substance; in your book were written, every one of them, the days that were formed for me, when as yet there was none of them. (Psalm 139:1-6;13-16)

So, follower of Jesus, your joyful task is to guard the deposit that has been entrusted to you. Like a secure display case in an art gallery that enables the beauty of a one-of-a-kind masterpiece to be expressed to the eyes of all observers, guarding the deposit entrusted to you enables you to express your identity as you were designed to do.

How in the world do we do that?

This is the question we will aim to answer in the remainder of this book.

IDENTIFY THE DEPOSIT

During the spring of 2016, I was completely miserable.

The questions that I had put off and postponed answering for years had become louder in my mind, and I could no longer ignore them. Who am I? What is my purpose?

I was no longer convinced that I was meant to continue in my career, but I couldn't think of anything else purposeful or meaningful that I wanted to do.

So, I descended into a period of deep searching and introspection. I was determined to answer these questions, no matter the cost. I had to know who I was. I had to know what was the purpose of my life. The voice inside me was screaming, "You matter!" but I could not explain why. Why did I matter?

Over the course of the following year, I endured a wilderness search for meaning and purpose. I spent hours crying out to God, begging Him to show me my purpose. The question kept me awake at night. It distracted me at work. It kept me from being present-minded with other people. I wrote countless pages in my journal, describing my thoughts and feelings.

In God's great kindness, He began to reveal answers to me. When I stopped screaming and began listening, He revealed my essence to me. He overwhelmed me with His gentle, fatherly voice. He whispered to me, "You are my beloved son in whom I am well-pleased," and "My delight is in you."

For a long time, that is all He gave me.

He wanted me to understand and *enjoy* my essence before showing me anything more.

Boy, did I enjoy it! It is an amazing thing to experience a father's blessing. So many deep desires are touched. This is what I was made for.

Over time, I began to look beyond my essence, *not for purpose or meaning* (I had all the purpose and meaning I could ever ask for, and more, from basking in my essence as a child of God), but for the delight of being my Father's son. I knew there were many things entrusted to me, and I wanted to discover practically what God wanted me to do with them. Now that God had firmly answered the question "Who am I?" in my mind and heart, I could begin to explore practically what I should do with my time, talents, and energy. I felt like my eight-year-old son when he wakes up in the morning with a smile on his face and says, "Good morning, Dad! What are we going to do today?"

This chapter is about the process God took me through to identify my deposit.

Knowing God, Knowing Myself

Expressing God's glory means looking like Him in the ways He made me to. It means seeking reversal of the ways that His glory in me has been tarnished and broken because of my sin and the sin of others in my life.

It is not possible to identify and maximize the unique ways that God has made us to reflect Him without first knowing God.

Knowing God's character enables us to imagine ourselves more clearly in His image and helps us to connect with those parts of His character that we were made to display.

God is powerful. He is authoritative. He is just. He is true. He is faithful. He is gentle. He is loving. He is kind. He is infinitely wise. He covers shame. He is trustworthy. He is compassionate. He is slow to become angry. He saves. He rescues. He delivers. He does not keep a record of wrongs against those who seek His forgiveness. He is radiant. He is breathtaking. He is a lawkeeper. He is a promise-keeper. He is generous. He is merciful. He is a provider. He hates inequity. He is a healer. He is a conqueror. He is perfect. He is peace. He is home. He is supremely valuable. He is present. He is intimate. He is supreme ruler. He is hope. He is life.

What part of God's transcendent beauty were you made to express?

Looking Inside

During my period of searching, there were several questions I began to use for reflection about how God made and equipped me uniquely. Here are the key questions I reflected on:

- What has God placed inside me that He wants me to offer to others?
    - How does God want me to express His beauty uniquely?
    - How does God want others to see Him in me?
- What are my primary passions?
    - What do I love to do?
    - What do I find myself dreaming about?
    - What evokes emotion in me?
    - If money were not a barrier, how would I spend my time? Why?

- What are the activities I enjoy most?
- What two or three words best describe a role that I am well-suited for?
  - What role or work do I long for?
- What are my healthy fears?
  - What are real dangers that I see earlier, more clearly, and more prominently than other people do and which I can help to steer other people safely away from?
- What are my unhealthy fears?
  - What are the areas which I'm tempted to be anxious and stressed about? Why?[4]

Answering these questions carefully and honestly without the negative pressure of wondering about my identity enabled me to begin to imagine how to use my time, talents, and energy in ways that maximize my expression of God's glory in my life.

Inviting Others In

An essential part of identifying the deposit God has entrusted to you to express is inviting others to be part of the identification process.

You will miss the most beautiful and wonderful parts you were designed to express if you seek to undertake this process on your own. Just as you were entrusted with unique expressions of God's glory, you were also given unique blind spots. It is a gentle and wonderful mercy from God that

Who Am I?

I don't see everything or know everything. He knows how impossible it would be for me to bear the burden of infinite knowledge and maintain integrity (let alone avoid exploding; my brain cannot fit all knowledge inside it).

If you want to seek maximum expression of God's beauty in your life, you *must* invite others to tell you what they see in you. Ask them to be honest and clear. Ask them to give you warnings, exhortations, admonitions, suggestions, and commands. Ask them to tell you things to avoid and things to pursue. Ask them to answer the questions above for themselves.

You don't have to ask everyone. However, you do need to approach people who know you and love you well enough to answer the questions honestly and perceptively.

Do this regularly. You will find that it is a refreshing and friendship-deepening process.

It is important to understand that not all words spoken to us about our identity, even by those that are close to us, will be accurate. You do not need to blindly receive all words spoken to you by those you trust. Prayerful discernment about what is true and what resonates as real and accurate in your spirit before God is essential. You should receive some things that are said to you, and you should reject other things that are said to you. Wisdom, humility, and prayer are your friends in this process.

What Am I Looking for?

So how will I know when I've found my unique deposit? What exactly am I looking for?

The Bible talks about spiritual gifts given to God's people that are specifically given for the purpose of building up or edifying His people. Another way of understanding this is the idea of "strengthening." If you have some particular trait or ability that is especially helpful and encouraging to others, which alleviates stress and anxiety, which brings energy and life, which brings healing and deliverance, which brings comfort and provision, which brings clarity and understanding, which removes loneliness and fear, which brings courage and hope, this is a gift you have been given to offer to others for their strengthening. It is part of the deposit that has been entrusted to you. Paul taught about spiritual gifts most explicitly in Romans 12 and I Corinthians 12. When you read these passages, don't focus primarily on the gifts that are listed by Paul in those passages. Instead, focus on the metaphor of the people of God as a body and each person as a body part with a unique and useful role to play that will enhance the functioning and health of the rest of the body.

Think of this process like climbing a mountain. The goal of the process is not to reach the top of the mountain but rather to enjoy (and share with others) the view along the way. The more you climb, the greater the self-awareness you will enjoy.

The deposit entrusted to you may or may not be connected to your vocation. It may or may not generate income for you. However, one thing is for sure: when other people see the deposit entrusted to you, they will be gladdened and strengthened. Through you, God will bring life and peace to those in your life.

Write It Down

In order to help you maintain focus and clarity, it can be very helpful to write down the knowledge that you gain through your identification process. I have done this for myself. Here is what I have written down so far:

Wim's life statement: To enjoy and be totally satisfied in God's heart and to strengthen others to enjoy and be totally satisfied in Him.

Wim's passions:
To promote the peace of God in relationships by seeking clarity, unity, and agreement (peacemaking)
To speak the truth with clarity at the right time (exhortation)
To call forth the gifts God has placed in each per-

son (father's heart to know and steward his child) (affirmation)
To minister the love of God to a people who have not yet tasted it or who have forgotten the taste of it (engagement)
To help people to taste and see afresh the delights of God (creative writing and teaching)
To help God's people be holy, healthy, and happy (Kingdom shepherding)

<u>Wim's field (area of spiritual work)</u>: Discouraged followers of Jesus, particularly ministers, who have forgotten their first love

<u>Wim's identity expression</u>: Happy prophet-shepherd

***

I am still changing and editing these things as I learn more about myself, but it has helped me to write these things down so that they can serve as a helpful compass in decision-making about how to spend my time, talents, and energy.

CULTIVATE THE DEPOSIT

*As each has received a gift, use it to serve one another, as good stewards of God's **varied grace**: whoever speaks, as one who speaks oracles of God; whoever serves, as one who serves by the strength that God supplies—in order that in everything God may be glorified through Jesus Christ. To him belong glory and dominion forever and ever. Amen.* (I Peter 4:10-11, emphasis added)

Though the process of identifying your unique deposit will take a lifetime, you will begin to understand what God has placed inside you to offer to those around you. When this begins to happen, you will be drawn to opportunities to express it. This is good! It is what you were made to do. Remember, God prepared this work in advance for you to do.

However, there will also arise obstacles and barriers. Remember too that sin and Satan will seek to keep you from expressing God's glory in your life. A passive mindset will not work well for you. You will need to be proactive. You will need to make sacrifices. You will need to learn to say "no" to many other things so that you can say "yes" to the things you were made to do.

Importantly, you will also need to invite others to help you learn to express your deposit in healthy ways. I heard a very wise man once say that everyone needs models, mentors, partners, and friends. He went on to define a model as someone in the past who has gone before you in your particular areas of strength and work; a mentor as someone in the present who has greater maturity and experience than you and can help to guide you in your area of strength and work; a partner as a peer with similar or complementary gifts and strengths whom you can work alongside in a mutually beneficial way; and a friend as someone who walks into your life and draws near to you in moments of pain when everyone else walks out.[5]

Prayer

Ask God for opportunities to express what God has placed in you. This has been so helpful to me. In so many moments of near-despair, I have cried out to God, "Father, why did you put these things in me? I know you didn't put them in me for no purpose! Show me the purpose for the things you have put inside me!"

He will show you. Indeed, He has not given you your unique set of abilities, experiences, relationships, possessions, gifts, and strengths for no purpose. He has very particular purposes in His mind to display His glory in you and through you. His purposes are not just good for Him at your expense. They are also good for you. You will enjoy the experience of discovering and expressing the gifts God has placed in you. Bringing gladness and joy to others will increase your own joy.

Practice

Be diligent and proactive in seeking opportunities to express the things God has placed inside you. Volunteer your time, talents, and energy. If someone asks you to help with something, find a way to say yes! If you see a need, offer to meet it.

Honestly examine how you spend your time and energy. Are there things that you do that are not helpful or productive? Are there things that are not life-giving? Are there things that are not honoring to God? Ask God (and invite others to help you stay accountable) to help you eliminate those things in order to free up time and energy to focus on the primary things God has placed inside you to offer those around you.

Feedback

Feedback is a necessary part of personal growth. The proverbs of the Bible offer great wisdom in this area.

> *Where there is no guidance, a people falls, but in an abundance of counselors there is safety.* (Proverbs 11:14)
>
> *Whoever walks with the wise becomes wise, but the companion of fools will suffer harm.* (Proverbs 13:20)
>
> *A soft answer turns away wrath, but a harsh word stirs up anger.* (Proverbs 15:1)
>
> *A rebuke goes deeper into a man of understanding than a hundred blows into a fool.* (Proverbs 17:10)
>
> *Pride goes before destruction, and a haughty spirit before a fall.* (Proverbs 16:18)
>
> *Better is open rebuke than hidden love. Faithful are the wounds of a friend; profuse are the kisses of an enemy.* (Proverbs 27:5-6)
>
> *Listen to advice and accept instruction, that you may gain wisdom in the future.* (Proverbs 19:20)

Solicit feedback from those around you, particularly from mentors, partners, and friends. Consider the feedback seriously. If it resonates with you as true and helpful, seek to implement it. If it causes you pain, consider whether the pain is from offense you have wrongfully taken. It may be that the feedback is true and good but has caused you offense because you have allowed pride to gain a place in your heart. If that is the case, eliminate pride from your heart (use your weapons!), and thank your friend for having the courage to speak the truth.

I feel some shame as I write this, recalling the moments in my past when I bristled at helpful and well-intentioned feedback that I received from loving friends. I have not always been gracious in receiving feedback.

Here are some helpful tips for receiving feedback that I seek to implement in my own life:

- Let people know that you welcome feedback. Regularly soliciting and welcoming feedback will help you be more open to receiving it and will help others have the courage to offer it.
- Cultivate an inner and outer posture of humility. Speak in a way that draws attention away from yourself. Downplay praise that you receive from others. Elevate the roles and accomplishments of others in your speaking.
- Remember that you don't need to receive all feedback provided to you. There is an art to graciously and thankfully acknowledging feedback that is provided to you without

fully receiving and agreeing with it. Be careful here! You do need to receive *some* feedback, and some of the feedback you may need to receive may not feel good immediately. Take time to slowly and genuinely reflect on the feedback. Consider, with prayer and possibly with counsel from others, whether the feedback contains an element of truth that you need to receive. Ask God to eliminate all pride and unhealthy barriers in your heart so that you can receive everything you need to receive and reject everything you need to reject. It is also helpful to wait to respond to the feedback provider until after you have made sure to eliminate any unhelpful self-defense and self-justification from your response. Aim for grace.

- Consider waiting to respond to the feedback provider until after you have made sure to eliminate any unhelpful self-defense and self-justification from your response. Aim for grace and humility.

Now we will turn to some practical matters that can bring discouragement and hamper the willingness and ability of followers of Jesus to earnestly seek expression of the unique deposit God placed inside each of His followers. We will examine the search for productivity, the barrier of scarcity, the difficulty and gift of personal weakness, and the feeling of foolishness.

REDEFINING PRODUCTIVITY

Let the favor of the Lord our God be upon us, and establish the work of our hands upon us; yes, establish the work of our hands!
(Psalm 90:17)

Productivity is a good thing. God made us for productivity. It is good to desire and seek productivity.

However, as with all aims and goals, it is vitally important to define the objective. This is particularly important in spiritual matters, which are inherently counter-cultural, counter-intuitive, and unnatural.

This is especially important in developed societies and cultures which have been heavily shaped by materialist thinking, defining reality in primarily physical and economic terms. It is so tempting and sometimes even relieving to define success in quantitative measures. Number of students enrolled (educational institutions), number of church attendees (churches), number of dollars raised (organizations that raise money through donations), amount of profit earned (for-profit enterprises), test scores (students), etc.

This is not entirely bad. Those objective measures can tell part of the story of what those organizations and people are involved with and what has been accomplished through their work. However, quantitative measures cannot tell the whole story any more than looking at someone's physical body enables you to know the whole person. There are things being accomplished in the spiritual realm which are beyond the ability of material and quantitative measures to fully describe.

So, I'd like to define "productivity" in the context of our discussion about expressing identity. What does it look like, in an ultimate or real sense, for Wim Codington to be productive? What does it look like for you to be productive? How can we measure productivity in the most holistic sense possible?

What Does God Want?

Before we define productivity, I'd like to explore together what is most important to God. Since my essence is "child of God," and since the work

God has prepared in advance for me should be an expression of my essence, what does it means to express my essence helpfully and productively? What does my Father expect of me?

The Bible teaches that God's ultimate aim in all He does is to display or magnify His own transcendent beauty, or glory. Here are some passages to demonstrate this:

> *I will say to the north, Give up, and to the south, Do not withhold; bring my sons from afar and my daughters from the end of the earth, everyone who is called by my name, whom I created **for my glory**, whom I formed and made.* (Isaiah 43:6-7, emphasis added)

God made His children for His glory.

> *For the earth will be filled with the **knowledge of the glory of the Lord** as the waters cover the sea.* (Habakkuk 2:14, emphasis added)

God's aim is to fill the earth with knowledge of His glory.

> *For from him and through him and to him are all things. **To him be glory** forever. Amen.* (Romans 11:36, emphasis added)

God is the origin, sustainer, and end of all things, all for the expression of His glory.

> *And I will harden Pharaoh's heart, and he will*

> *pursue them, and **I will get glory** over Pharaoh and all his host, and the Egyptians shall know that I am the Lord....* (Exodus 14:4, emphasis added)

Even in the events of rebellion against God, God is moving in the events to reveal His glory. God always has the last word.

We can see that God clearly has a passion for His glory. This is natural and good, as many others have so powerfully demonstrated in their writing, because God is the highest and most valuable being. If God cared more about the glory and beauty of something other than Himself, it would mean that He is not the most valuable being. In other words, He would not be God. This is not a bad thing. It is a good thing.

How does this impact my daily living and choosing? Is God some kind of cosmic director that always moves the events of the world for His glory without expecting that we also participate in working toward His glory?

Is God the only one that needs to care about God's glory, or should I also care about God's glory?

Let's examine some of the teaching of Jesus and Paul in order to answer this question.

> But ***I do not account my life of any value nor as precious to myself, if only I may*** *finish my course and the ministry that I received from the Lord Jesus, to **testify to the gospel of the grace of God***.

(Acts 20:24, emphasis added)

Paul clearly defined the value of His life only in terms of communicating (testifying) about the good news of God's grace given in Jesus. This was his personal definition of success.

Was Paul just a special case? After all, he had a very unique assignment from God in building the early church after the ascension of Jesus. What about you and me?

A few more passages from Paul and Jesus help answer this question.

> *For it is all for your sake, so that as grace extends to more and more people it may increase thanksgiving, **to the glory of God**.* (2 Corinthians 4:15, emphasis added)

In this wonderful passage about the purpose of his affliction and sacrifices made on behalf of the Corinthian church, Paul clearly shows that his aim in his ministry to the Corinthians is to extend grace to them and through them to others, to increase thankfulness and give glory to God.

> *So, whether you eat or drink, or whatever you do, **do all to the glory of God**.* (I Corinthians 10:31, emphasis added)

This is an even simpler and clearer statement from Paul to the Corinthian church. The aim of all they do ought to be to enhance God's glory.

> *The one who speaks on his own authority seeks his own glory; but **the one who seeks the glory of him who sent him is true**, and in him there is no falsehood.* (John 7:18, emphasis added)

Jesus, answering an attack on His own authenticity and trustworthiness, shows that the aim of His teaching is to seek God's glory.

> *You are the salt of the earth, but if salt has lost its taste, how shall its saltiness be restored? It is no longer good for anything except to be thrown out and trampled under people's feet. "You are the light of the world. A city set on a hill cannot be hidden. Nor do people light a lamp and put it under a basket, but on a stand, and it gives light to all in the house. In the same way, let your light shine before others, so **that they may see your good works and give glory to your Father** who is in heaven.* (Matthew 5:13-16, emphasis added)

This teaching of Jesus gives two wonderful metaphors about how followers of Jesus should think about our living: saltiness (enhancing the flavors found in food) and light (enhancing the beauty found in a place). The aim of our living ought to be to enhance God's glory (flavor and beauty) through our actions.

So, we have seen that God's ultimate purpose in all He does is to maximize His glory. We have also seen that this was the purpose of Jesus and of Paul in their own work. We have also seen that this is what is expected of all other followers of Jesus.

Defining Godly Productivity

Now we are finally ready to define Godly productivity.

Wim's definition: *Godly productivity is anything a person does that helps other human beings to see God's nature more gloriously.*

This can involve all sorts of work. God made everything for His glory, so everything He made can legitimately be used to display His glory.

This requires significant unpacking, because there are numerous negative influences that seek to prevent God's glory from being displayed. All of these negative influences can be traced back to sin and Satan.

If you are an artist, but if you do not help those who see your art look past you and see the God Who is the Originator of all beautiful things and Who Himself is the essence of Beauty, you may not be helping others to see God more gloriously.

If you are a businessman, but if you do not help your clients and colleagues to look past your economic productivity and see the God Who created all good things and the capacity to make and enjoy wealth, you may not be helping others to see God more gloriously.

If you are a medical professional, but if you do not help your patients to look past your ability to help people heal, avoid pain and see the God Who made the capacity for healing and is Himself the healer,[6] you may not be helping others to see God more gloriously.

If you are a legal professional, but if you do not help your clients to look past your ability to help bring clarity and equity and see the God Who loves justice and will one day right every wrong and expose every lie, you may not be helping others to see God more gloriously.

If you are a caregiver, but if you do not help those you care for to look past your ability to bring comfort and rest and see the God Who offers rest and comfort in His presence, you may not be helping others to see God more gloriously.

If you are a builder, but if you do not help those who see and enjoy your buildings to look past your ability to create beautiful and useful structures that provide shelter and utility and see the God Who made all things and will one day call all of His children into an extravagant city to live in with Him forever, you may not be helping others to see God more gloriously.

If you care for animals or plants, but if you do not help the other people that enjoy the plants and animals that you care for to look past your ability to cultivate and care for them and see the God Who made all creation wonderfully diverse as a reflection of His kindness and creativity, you may not be helping others to see God more gloriously.

This is not just true for the primary or vocational ways that we spend our time. It is true for *all* ways that we spend our time. When we are pumping gas at the gas station, when we are loading up the grocery cart, when we are enjoying food at home, when we are with friends, when we are preparing for bed, how are we spending our time in ways that help others to see God in us?

I could go on, but I hope I have made my point. Godly productivity is more than just doing something well. It requires openly and explicitly directing any praise and recognition that results from well-doing toward God.

This requires using words. It is not enough to silently do things well. Speaking and writing about the God who created all things for His glory is necessary to help others make the connection between the good things you have produced and the One Who is the source of all good things.

When you open your mouth to respond to praise for your well-doing, take care that you give all recognition to God for the good that you do.

What About Me?

Self-care is an important dynamic to reflect on and to discuss with family and friends. We can't spend all of our waking hours in the presence of other people and meeting the needs of other people. All human beings require varying amounts of time alone in order to be healthy. When we are alone, are we spending our time in ways that bring spiritual, mental, emotional, and physical refreshment in a way that is life-giving (honoring the God Who gave us our bodies and intends for us to care for them as good stewards) but not self-indulgent (seeking physical pleasure as an end in itself)? These things require wisdom, because each person is different and has unique needs. The next chapter discusses the dynamic of scarcity of resources (including personal needs) and may be helpful for navigating limitations of physical and emotional energy.

What About "Unproductive" Days?

Everyone has days on which they feel they have not accomplished anything.

This morning, I babysat two disabled children so that their mother could have a break and enjoy some time with others. As I sat caring for the girls, thinking about all of the "productive" things I could be doing instead, it occurred to me that helping my friend to have a break from her tiresome job of being a stay at home mother is just as productive as balancing my checkbook or teaching a class or mowing my lawn, and perhaps even more. The clarifying question I want to ask myself at the end of a day or a task is "Did other people experience more of God's power and love because of what I did today?"

Let this question guide you, more than checking things off of your to-do list, more than measuring the praise you receive from other people, and more than the dollars you see in your bank account.

If people have seen Jesus in you and through you, you have done well.

REDEFINING SCARCITY

All of us experience limitations of our energy, time, and other resources. The limitations can be confoundingly frustrating, leaving us with a feeling of never quite "arriving" at our goal and also leaving us susceptible to the pitfall of comparing ourselves with other people, which usually only increases the feeling of frustration.

Growing older brings additional limitations in physical energy and mobility which can add to the frustrations brought by scarce energy and time and the ever-increasing dependence on other people for even the most basic physical needs.

Many of us think that we really need to maximize our goals is personal autonomy. We want to be able to accomplish our goals with unlimited energy, time, resources, and independence. When our autonomy is encroached upon, the feeling of frustration creeps in.

Defining and overcoming scarcity

I'd like to show in this chapter that the way to maximize our expression of God's glory in us is not to maximize our personal autonomy but rather to maximize our faith in God.

First, though, we need to define scarcity.

Wim's definition: *Scarcity is a limitation of access to resources.*

This is different from an economist's definition of scarcity, which is a limitation of the actual resources themselves, rather than a limitation of *access* to the resources.

In God's economy, there is no limitation of actual resources. He made all things from nothing and is able to create and multiply out of nothing. He is outside of time and created time itself. He is able to alter the created dynamics of time and space and has done so many times in response to the prayers of His people.[7] God is the God of abundance. He has abundant time and resources. Let's look at a couple of passages that teach this truth.

> *Now to him **who is able to do far more abundantly than all that we ask or think**, according*

> *to the power at work within us, to him be glory in the church and in Christ Jesus throughout all generations, forever and ever. Amen.* (Ephesians 3:20-21, emphasis added)

> *But do not overlook this one fact, beloved, that **with the Lord one day is as a thousand years, and a thousand years as one day.*** (2 Peter 3:8, emphasis added)

The reason He has allowed an apparent limitation of resources that is overcome through faith and prayer is that He receives great glory from the faith-filled prayers of His people that look to Him as Provider. The only true scarcity is the limitation of human faith, which prevents us from accessing God's abundant and limitless resources.

As you can tell by now from my writing, I don't want you to take my word for it. I want you to see this for yourself in the Bible. So, let's look to some passages to see how important prayerful faith in God's abundance and goodness is for unlocking his provision for our needs.

> *Therefore I tell you, **do not be anxious about your life, what you will eat or what you will drink, nor about your body, what you will put on.** Is not life more than food, and the body more than clothing? Look at the birds of the air: they neither sow nor reap nor gather into barns, and yet your heavenly Father feeds them. Are you not of more value than they? And which of you by being anx-*

*ious can add a single hour to his span of life? And why are you anxious about clothing? Consider the lilies of the field, how they grow: they neither toil nor spin, yet I tell you, even Solomon in all his glory was not arrayed like one of these. But if God so clothes the grass of the field, which today is alive and tomorrow is thrown into the oven, will he not much more clothe you, O you of little faith? Therefore do not be anxious, saying, "What shall we eat?" or "What shall we drink?" or "What shall we wear?" For the Gentiles seek after all these things, and **your heavenly Father knows that you need them all. But seek first the kingdom of God and his righteousness, and all these things will be added to you.** Therefore **do not be anxious about tomorrow**, for tomorrow will be anxious for itself. **Sufficient for the day is its own trouble.*** (Matthew 6:25-34, emphasis added)

These words, spoken by Jesus, were meant to show by comparison with flowers and birds, how silly it is to doubt God's future provision for us human beings, who are far more valuable to Him than plants and animals. Notice that Jesus gently chides the "little faith" of his listeners and encourages a "daily bread" faith, asking God to provide for today's needs and not wondering about the needs of the future but instead trusting that God will provide for future needs at the right time and in the right way. Faith in God's loving intention to provide unlocks His provision.

> *And behold, some people brought to him a paralytic, lying on a bed. And when **Jesus saw their faith**, he said to the paralytic, "Take heart, my son; your sins are forgiven." And behold, some of the scribes said to themselves, "This man is blaspheming." But Jesus, knowing their thoughts, said, "Why do you think evil in your hearts? For which is easier, to say, 'Your sins are forgiven,' or to say, 'Rise and walk'? But that you may know that the Son of Man has authority on earth to forgive sins"—he then said to the paralytic—"Rise, pick up your bed and go home." And he rose and went home. When the crowds saw it, they were afraid, and they glorified God, who had given such authority to men.* (Matthew 9:2-8, emphasis added)

In this story, Jesus forgave the sin *and* healed the legs of a paralytic in order to authenticate His power which was clearly unlocked through the faith of the people who brought the paralytic for healing.

> *Jesus turned, and seeing her he said, "Take heart, daughter; **your faith has made you well**." And instantly the woman was made well.* (Matthew 9:22, emphasis added)

Once again, faith unleashed the healing power of Jesus.

> *And when they came to the crowd, a man came*

> up to him and, kneeling before him, said, "Lord, have mercy on my son, for he has seizures and he suffers terribly. For often he falls into the fire, and often into the water. And I brought him to your disciples, and they could not heal him." And Jesus answered, "O faithless and twisted generation, how long am I to be with you? How long am I to bear with you? Bring him here to me." And Jesus rebuked the demon, and it came out of him, and the boy was healed instantly. Then the disciples came to Jesus privately and said, "**Why could we not cast it out?" He said to them, "Because of your little faith**. For truly, I say to you, if you have faith like a grain of mustard seed, you will say to this mountain, 'Move from here to there,' and it will move, and nothing will be impossible for you." (Matthew 17:14-21, emphasis added)

This story is striking because Jesus' disciples themselves who had seen Jesus perform miracles previously, struggled to have faith. This is both comforting to those of us that struggle to have faith (even Jesus' disciples struggled) and alarming since it means that everyone, even the mighty disciples and others who have been eyewitnesses to great demonstrations of God's power, are susceptible to the plague of doubt. Jesus clearly said that the disciples were unable to cast out the demon because of their little faith. Let us beware of unbelief and root it out from our hearts.

> He went away from there and came to his home-

> *town, and his disciples followed him. And on the Sabbath he began to teach in the synagogue, and many who heard him were astonished, saying, "Where did this man get these things? What is the wisdom given to him? How are such mighty works done by his hands? Is not this the carpenter, the son of Mary and brother of James and Joses and Judas and Simon? And are not his sisters here with us?" And they took offense at him. And Jesus said to them, "A prophet is not without honor, except in his hometown and among his relatives and in his own household." **And he could do no mighty work there**, except that he laid his hands on a few sick people and healed them. **And he marveled because of their unbelief**....* (Mark 6:1-6, emphasis added)

This is another striking story because it shows that Jesus Himself *could not* demonstrate His power in a mighty way because of the unbelief of the people in His hometown. This story clearly shows that lack of faith prevents access to God's power.

> *Now faith is the assurance of things hoped for, the conviction of things not seen. For by it the people of old received their commendation. By faith we understand that the universe was created by the word of God, so that what is seen was not made out of things that are visible.... And what more shall I say? For **time would fail me to tell of Gideon, Barak, Samson, Jephthah, of David and***

> *Samuel and the prophets— who through faith conquered kingdoms, enforced justice, obtained promises, stopped the mouths of lions, quenched the power of fire, escaped the edge of the sword, were made strong out of weakness, became mighty in war, put foreign armies to flight.* (Hebrews 11:1-3; 32-34, emphasis added)

Stories of power increase faith. It is so important for followers of Jesus to share stories of God's provision and power openly with one another. Hebrews 11 is a compelling list of stories of God's faith-enabled power in the lives of many of His people over the course of history. The people in the list were not strong and mighty in their own right. They did not own vast resources. Rather, they had faith in God's abundant power and goodness. Because of their faith, God used them to do amazing things. So it can be with you!

> *If any of you lacks wisdom,* **let him ask God, who gives generously to all without reproach, and it will be given him. But let him ask in faith, with no doubting,** *for the one who doubts is like a wave of the sea that is driven and tossed by the wind. For that person must not suppose that he will receive anything from the Lord; he is a double-minded man, unstable in all his ways.* (James 1:5-8, emphasis added)

We have a clear warning against doubt in this passage. We must be compassionate with those who doubt; we must not condemn them. Everyone struggles with doubt at various times. However, we must not condone doubt itself. Doubt is evil and causes God's power to be thwarted. Do not doubt. Ask God, without doubting, for His abundant provision for the particular needs you have, and you'll be amazed at how He answers.

One final reminder, in case you need convincing of God's goodness and power:

> *He who did not spare his own Son but gave him up for us all, how **will he not also with him graciously give us all things**?* (Romans 8:32, emphasis added)

Don't forget! God gave His own Son for you. Of course He will give you everything else in addition to His Son that you could possibly need or desire in the fullness of time.

Follower of Jesus: When you feel poor, pray. When you feel hungry, pray. When the pantry is empty, pray. When you overdraft your bank account, pray. When you can't take another step, pray. When you have nothing good left in you, pray. When you feel utterly alone and desperate, pray. Do not doubt God's goodness or power. Cry out to Him with confidence. He will answer you like a lion, and you'll be amazed by His tender, mighty, personal, generous provision. He will not leave you.

Abundance and Need

On some days you will experience God's abundance fully and clearly. On other days, you'll feel your poverty more deeply than you ever have before.

This is a common experience of followers of Jesus. On the abundant days, celebrate God's goodness with all your might, and take advantage of the energy, money, time, and other abundant resources! When I am working on a writing project and I have a day full of inspiration, I take full advantage! I celebrate the inspiration and try to put it to good use. If I have a day on which I feel completely alone and aimless and am tempted to despair, I do not try to attempt big things. I just try to focus on the next thing in front of me. Make lunch. Respond to emails. Do tasks that don't require too much emotional energy. Above all, cry out to God to help me, and meditate on His promises. He has a way of bringing us out of despondence through the power of His Word, and He often surprises us with goodness in the midst of our deep need.

The apostle Paul experienced perhaps a greater change in altitude between mountaintop and valley experiences than almost any other follower of Jesus. Here is how Paul approached these experiences:

> *...I have learned in whatever situation I am to be content. I know how to be brought low, and I know how to abound.* In any and every circumstance, I have learned the secret of facing plenty and hunger, abundance and need. I can do all things through him who strengthens me.... *And my God will supply every need of yours according to his riches in glory in Christ Jesus.* (Philippians 4:11-13,19, emphasis added)

Paul's secret was to trust His loving Father who had always provided in the past and promised to always provide in the future according to His riches.

Let this be your secret too!

EMBRACING WEAKNESS

*F**or I consider that the sufferings of this present time are not worth comparing with the glory that is to be revealed to us. For the creation waits with eager longing for the revealing of the sons of God. For the creation was subjected to futility, not willingly, but because of him who subjected it, in hope that the creation itself will be set free from its bondage to corruption and obtain the freedom of the glory of the children of God. For we know that the whole creation has been groaning together in the pains of childbirth until now. And not only the creation, but we ourselves, who have the firstfruits of the Spirit, groan inwardly as we wait eagerly for adoption as sons, the redemption of our bodies. For in this hope we were saved. Now hope that is seen is not hope. For who hopes for what he sees? But if we hope for*

> *what we do not see, we wait for it with patience.*
> (Romans 8:18-25)

Any attempt at self-actualization on this side of heaven, no matter how much is accomplished, no matter how much beauty is expressed, and no matter how much God blesses it, will still contain an element of futility and frustration.

We will not completely overcome sin or its effects in our lives until we die and experience the last leg of our liberation from the bondage of sin. In addition, the rest of creation is in the same boat as us.

We cannot always do things we are good at. We cannot always do things we enjoy. We cannot always do things that are easy for us.

Linear thinkers will need to do brainstorming.
Brainstormers will need to follow detailed, step-by-step instructions.
People with low energy will need to do things that require meaningful energy.
People with high energy will need to do things that require long and slow concentration.
Introverts will need to engage with people.
Extroverts will need to spend time alone.
Visionaries will need to give detailed feedback and make detailed decisions.
Process-oriented people will need to look ahead and identify future needs to begin planning for today.

Conflict-averse people will need to resolve disputes.
Fighters will need to provide encouragement.

When we are faced with circumstances that are difficult for us, how will we respond?

There are two passages that are so helpful to me when I am faced with circumstances that are difficult.

> *And we know that for those who love God all things work together for good, for those who are called according to his purpose.* (Romans 8:28)

God has used this incredible promise from Romans to enable me to win many battles in my life against fear of the future and fear of my own weakness. Think of it: every single thing that happens to God's people will turn out for our good! Our problems, our suffering, our mistakes, our exposure, our confessions, our stumbling, our failures, and our limitations: all of these will produce blessings for us. Wow! What a promise! What a truth! What a reality!

> *Three times I pleaded with the Lord about this, that it should leave me. But he said to me, "**My grace is sufficient for you, for my power is made perfect in weakness**." Therefore **I will boast all the more gladly of my weaknesses**, so that the power of Christ may rest upon me. For the sake of Christ, then, **I am content with weaknesses**, in-*

sults, hardships, persecutions, and calamities. For **when I am weak, then I am strong.** (2 Corinthians 12:8-10, emphasis added)

This passage is a very personal account from Paul about circumstances in his life which caused him great pain and suffering. He asked God to deliver him from his suffering, but God had an even greater purpose in mind for this particular suffering of Paul. God intended to show Paul that God's power is perfected (manifested most fully and brightly) in the presence of weakness.

If a strong man wins a fight, who will marvel at God's power in the man? Who will say, "The power of Christ was clearly resting on that man!" No one! The strength to win the fight would seem to have come from the man himself. However, if a weak man engages in a battle that looks impossible for him to win, clings to Christ in prayer and faith, and experiences victory, God's power is made perfect because it is put on display in the weak man. The strong man was no less empowered by God than the weak man, for his strength was created by God. However, God's power is displayed with the greatest clarity and prominence in the presence of weakness.

Therefore, embrace your weakness and your suffering. Ask God to shine through you. Ask God to overcome your weakness through His power and to make a name for Himself through you. He will do it. That kind of prayer brings Him great honor!

EMBRACING FOOLISHNESS

There is something in the heart of natural human beings that deeply fears foolishness.

I feel this with my entire being. When I start a conversation with nearly everyone other than the people in my closest inner circle, my natural inclination is to seek to impress. I want to make someone say, "Wow, Wim is impressive!"

This inner inclination says "self-actualization happens through self-assertiveness."

The dirty truth about this type of behavior is that it leads to shallower and hollower selves. It does not increase authenticity; it does not lead to self-actualization.

It leads to self-destruction.

The pathway to self-actualization, in God's infinite wisdom, must include embracing foolishness.

Wisdom is an inclination to do what is right.

Foolishness is the opposite of wisdom.

Why then does self-actualization require embracing foolishness?

The kind of foolishness that leads to self-actualization is foolishness in the eyes of the world. The world, as the Bible talks about it, means the kingdom of darkness that is ruled by Satan.

Satan's kingdom advocates self-assertiveness, led by Satan's own example. As we saw in the Ezekiel passage that described Satan's fall from glory, Satan's preoccupation with his own impressiveness was his downfall.

To the world, it is utterly foolish to be self-deprecating. It is very, very foolish to not be polished, accomplished, credentialed, titled, professional, important, and impressive.

And yet, this is the kind of foolishness God expects of His children on the path to self-actualization. Godly foolishness is an inclination to act for a single audience (God) and to protect His glory by avoiding personal attention.

Let's look at a few Bible passages where we see this

kind of foolishness. I believe the clearest place is Paul's teaching in his letter to the Corinthian church:

> *Where is the one who is wise? Where is the scribe? Where is the debater of this age? Has not God made foolish the wisdom of the world? For since, in the wisdom of God, the world did not know God through wisdom, it pleased God through the folly of what we preach to save those who believe. For Jews demand signs and Greeks seek wisdom, but we preach Christ crucified, a stumbling block to Jews and folly to Gentiles, but to those who are called, both Jews and Greeks, Christ the power of God and the wisdom of God.* ***For the foolishness of God is wiser than men, and the weakness of God is stronger than men.*** *For consider your calling, brothers:* ***not many of you were wise*** *according to worldly standards,* ***not many were powerful, not many were of noble birth.*** *But* ***God chose what is foolish*** *in the world to shame the wise;* ***God chose what is weak*** *in the world to shame the strong;* ***God chose what is low and despised*** *in the world, even things that are not, to bring to nothing things that are, so that no human being might boast in the presence of God. And because of him you are in Christ Jesus, who became to us wisdom from God, righteousness and sanctification and redemption, so that, as it is written, "Let the one who boasts, boast in the Lord."* (I Corinthians 1:20-31, emphasis added)

This passage contains a striking contrast between the wisdom of the world and the wisdom of God, which appears as foolishness to the world. It is foolish to the world because this kind of wisdom is not self-exalting; rather, it is Jesus-exalting. This is the definition of true wisdom. In this passage, Paul seeks to encourage followers of Jesus that Jesus is all we need as a carrying card to authenticate and empower us in the work of telling others about Jesus. Jesus is enough.

> *Now he told a parable to those who were invited, when he noticed how they chose the places of honor, saying to them, "When you are invited by someone to a wedding feast, do not sit down in a place of honor, lest someone more distinguished than you be invited by him, and he who invited you both will come and say to you, 'Give your place to this person,' and then you will begin with shame to take the lowest place. But when you are invited, **go and sit in the lowest place**, so that when your host comes he may say to you, 'Friend, move up higher.' Then you will be honored in the presence of all who sit at table with you. **For everyone who exalts himself will be humbled, and he who humbles himself will be exalted**." (Luke 14:7-11, emphasis added)*

This passage contains the same paradox in the form of a parable that makes sense in daily life. No one wants to be around a person that asserts himself over others in public places, and seeking to honor oneself can lead to shame. However, honoring others and humbling yourself creates the relational space and desire in the hearts of others (especially in God's heart) to lift you up and let you share in the honor of King Jesus, after sharing in His humbling.

> *...So David went and brought up the ark of God from the house of Obed-edom to the city of David with rejoicing. And when those who bore the ark of the Lord had gone six steps, he sacrificed an ox and a fattened animal. And **David danced before the Lord with all his might**. And David was wearing a linen ephod. So David and all the house of Israel brought up the ark of the Lord with shouting and with the sound of the horn. As the ark of the Lord came into the city of David, Michal the daughter of Saul looked out of the window and saw King David leaping and dancing before the Lord, and she despised him in her heart. And they brought in the ark of the Lord and set it in its place, inside the tent that David had pitched for it. And David offered burnt offerings and peace offerings before the Lord. And when David had finished offering the burnt offerings and the peace offerings, he blessed the people in the name of the Lord of hosts and distributed among all the people, the whole multitude of Israel, both men and women, a cake of bread, a portion of meat, and a cake of raisins to each one. Then all the*

*people departed, each to his house. And David returned to bless his household. But Michal the daughter of Saul came out to meet David and said, "How the king of Israel honored himself today, uncovering himself today before the eyes of his servants' female servants, as one of the vulgar fellows shamelessly uncovers himself!" And David said to Michal, "It was before the Lord, who chose me above your father and above all his house, to appoint me as prince over Israel, the people of the Lord—and **I will celebrate before the Lord. I will make myself yet more contemptible than this, and I will be abased** in your eyes. But by the female servants of whom you have spoken, by them I shall be held in honor."* (2 Samuel 6:12-22, emphasis added)

This passage contains a wonderful story of King David, the most powerful and beloved king of Israel, debasing himself publicly. What was shameful about David's behavior was *not* that he uncovered parts of his body that should not be uncovered (he did not do that). Rather, what was shameful, in a worldly sense, was that he did not conduct himself in a "kingly" or "regal" way. He was not dignified. Rather, he was undignified. He was dancing before the Lord with all his might!

What a picture! Are you willing to dance before the Lord with all your might, as for an audience of one single Person?

There are other stories of self-abasement in the Bible, including the story of Jesus taking the form of a servant and washing the feet of His disciples (John 13), something unthinkable in the culture of Jesus' day because of its clear message of self-abasement. God asked the prophet Ezekiel to lie on his side publicly for months at a time and to bake food publicly using his own excrement as a sign of the defiling of God's people caused by sin (Ezekiel 4). God asked the prophet Hosea to marry an unfaithful prostitute in order to send a message to God's people about their unfaithfulness to God (Hosea 1). God asked the apostle Paul to turn his back on his prestigious worldly education and credentials (Philippians 3) and become a lowly tentmaker in order to fund his ministry of traveling from place to place to tell others about Jesus.

Follower of Jesus: throw off the chains of self-consciousness. Let go of worldly credentials and let Jesus be your first and last credential. Be self-forgetful and Christ-conscious. Embrace foolishness, and others will begin to see in you the wisdom of God as only you were designed to express it.

THE FINAL SECRET

There is a final paradox that must be grasped in order for this whole identity thing to make sense in your life. Here is the paradox:

Embracing essence enables expression.

You will be sorely tempted to focus on expression when defining your identity. This is the danger of social media and image management. Defining our identity by what others see in us will increase hollowness inside us and will cause us to move farther and farther away from what God intended others to see in us.

You will also be tempted to look to personality awareness tools such as the enneagram to assist in defining the essence of your identity. *Do not do this.* Those tools are helpful in understanding how you were uniquely made to *express* your identity, but they are not your *essence*. "Child of God" is your essence. "United to Jesus and reflecting His image" is your essence. "Filled with the Spirit" is your essence.

You will also be tempted to define the essence of your identity and that of others by your weaknesses. *Do not do this.* Remember that you and other followers of Jesus are a new creation in Jesus (2 Corinthians 5). When you look at yourself and at other followers of Jesus, look at your weaknesses as superficial and temporary blemishes, expressions of the old you that is passing away, which God can and will overcome at the right time. Do not let them define your sense of self or how you see others.

The secret to maximizing our expression of God's glory that others see in our lives is to embrace the essence of our identity. That is, embrace God Himself as our Father, our Lover, our Friend, our Maker, our Creator, our Redeemer, our Healer, our Strong Tower, our Refuge, our Shelter, our Righteousness, our Victory, our Sustainer, our Helper, our Everything.

One of the greatest psalms in the Bible to bring us back to this place of delighting in God is Psalm 16:

> *Preserve me, O God, for in you I take refuge. I say to the Lord, "You are my Lord; **I have no good apart from you.**" As for the saints in the land, they are the excellent ones, in whom is all my delight. The sorrows of those who run after another*

god shall multiply; their drink offerings of blood I will not pour out or take their names on my lips. **The Lord is my chosen portion and my cup; you hold my lot.** *The lines have fallen for me in pleasant places; indeed, I have a beautiful inheritance. I bless the Lord who gives me counsel; in the night also my heart instructs me. I have set the Lord always before me; because he is at my right hand, I shall not be shaken.* **Therefore my heart is glad, and my whole being rejoices; my flesh also dwells secure.** *For you will not abandon my soul to Sheol, or let your holy one see corruption.* **You make known to me the path of life, in your presence there is fullness of joy; at your right hand are pleasures forevermore.** (Psalm 16, emphasis added)

Follower of Jesus: Your pathway to self-actualization, to maximizing the expression of your essence, and to displaying the deposit entrusted to you, can only be to embrace Jesus with all your heart, soul, strength, and mind. Relax in His love.

You will find that His Spirit will fill you so full that you will overflow, and others will experience living water through you.

THE FINAL CHARGE

Are you ready to self-actualize? Do you feel you have all the tools in your toolbelt? Are you excited and ready to go?

Go in the strength that God provides!

Are you really ready? Do you really know who you are?

When you are ridiculed, will you remember who you are?
When you are rejected, will you remember who you are?
When you are impoverished, will you remember who you are?
When you are endangered, will you remember who you are?
When your family is killed, will you remember who you are?
When your health leaves you, will you remember who you are?

When your bank account is empty, will you remember who you are?

When your friends betray you, will you remember who you are?

When your work fails, will you remember who you are?

When your life is threatened, will you remember who you are?

When you feel you know the deposit in you and are ready and willing to offer it, but no one else seems to care, will you remember who you are?

God's power in you is infinitely bigger than you realize, and He may, in His sovereign wisdom, allow you to experience great difficulty as part of His larger plan to raise you up in power in a great display of His glory. This will be for your good, not just for God's good.

Sometimes God leads His children into the wilderness for a season of sharpening, deepening, honing, and pruning. This happened for many of the most mighty prophets in the Bible including David, Paul, and Jesus. The wilderness is always purposeful. God wants to do something *in* you before He raises you up to do things *through* you. He will most certainly raise you up in a mighty way. He did not put your gifts inside you for no purpose. He plans for you to use your gifts in a mighty way that will bring great glory to Himself, blessing to others, and pleasure to you.

Trust Him. Lean heavily on Him. Do not ever, ever, ever forget that you are a child of God and a sheep in the sheepfold of Jesus, the Good Shepherd. He is with you, mighty to save. His arm is very long. He will reach for you and pluck you out of the deepest dungeons and place you high upon a rock, so that your head will be lifted up above all of your enemies. It is just a matter of time.

> ***Fear not, little flock, for it is your Father's good pleasure to give you the kingdom****.* (Luke 12:32, emphasis added)

> ***My sheep hear my voice**, and I know them, and they follow me. I give them eternal life, and **they will never perish, and no one will snatch them out of my hand**. My Father, who has given them to me, is greater than all, and **no one is able to snatch them out of the Father's hand**.* (John 10:27-29, emphasis added)

> *What then shall we say to these things? **If God is for us, who can be against us**? He who did not spare his own Son but gave him up for us all, how will he not also with him graciously give us all things? **Who shall bring any charge against God's elect**? It is God who justifies. Who is to condemn? Christ Jesus is the one who died—more than that, who was raised—who is at the right hand of God, who indeed is interceding for us. **Who shall separate us from the love of Christ**? Shall tribulation, or distress, or persecution, or*

famine, or nakedness, or danger, or sword? As it is written, "For your sake we are being killed all the day long; we are regarded as sheep to be slaughtered." No, **in all these things we are more than conquerors through him who loved us.** *For I am sure that* **neither death nor life, nor angels nor rulers, nor things present nor things to come, nor powers, nor height nor depth, nor anything else in all creation, will be able to separate us from the love of God in Christ Jesus our Lord.** (Romans 8:31-39)

POSSIBLE OBJECTIONS TO THE MESSAGE IN THIS BOOK

It is important to me to engage in helpful conversations about relevant topics in order to enable helpful change. Unanswered objections stop conversations and threaten helpful change. So, I have attempted to identify and respond to possible objections to the message of this book.

I don't expect that I have identified all possible objections, so I have included contact information at the end of the book so that we can continue the conversation. If I have said things in this book that are untrue, unhelpful, or incomplete, please contact me so that I can hear your feedback.

Objection one: This is just Enlightenment-inspired individualism

This objection might see the similarities between the individualistic impulses that emerged from the Enlightenment age of Europe which promoted the moral worth of the individual and inspired liberalism, hedonism, humanism, and many other philosophical streams of thought.

In contrast with individualism, the Bible teaches that we ought to put others before ourselves, seeking personal surrender to God and humility as the primary ethical standards. How then can a book about self-actualization and individual identity co-exist with and follow the Bible's teaching?

The answer, in my view, is in the paradox I presented at the end of the book. The greater self-forgetfulness we practice, resting in the essence of our God-given identity, the greater the glory that others will see in us. It is not self-exalting to seek to display God's glory in our lives. It is God-exalting. In the process of exalting God and pursuing humility, we ourselves will participate in God's glory.

> *Humble yourselves, therefore, under the mighty hand of God so that at the proper time he may*

exalt you…. (I Peter 5:6)

In addition to the emphasis on personal humility, which contrasts with Enlightenment-inspired self-assertiveness, the Bible teaches that there are different individual gifts that are to be identified and expressed for the good of the people of God. Romans 12 and I Corinthians 12 clearly teach that individual people have received gifts (deposits) to be offered (expressed).

In the end, the difference between true self-actualization of followers of Jesus and all other attempts at self-actualization is that true self-actualization of followers of Jesus makes God look great. It enhances His glory. It prompts God to beam with approval, and it prompts others to worship God.

Objection two: God has not shown us the future, so how can we know what He intends us to express of Himself?

This is an understandable question. After all, God's ways are higher than our ways and His thoughts than our thoughts,[8] right? Who has known the unsearchable mind of the Lord?[9]

Yes, these things are true in a sense. We should not presume to understand all of God's purposes in the events of our lives; if we did, we would not need faith. However, we can understand *some* of God's purpose, and we should seek to understand fuller and deeper meaning in the events of our lives in order that we may live more and more single-mindedly. He does not withhold understanding from those who seek it.

God will always retain the element of surprise as a way of delighting us and gently reminding us to stay humble and dependent on Him. However, this does not mean that God is completely unknowable or that we have no compass to direct us. With God's Spirit in us, God's desires are sufficiently knowable and followable.

> *For this commandment that I command you today is not too hard for you, neither is it far off. It is not in heaven, that you should say, "Who will ascend to heaven for us and bring it to us, that we may hear it and do it?" Neither is it beyond the sea, that you should say, "Who will go over the sea for us and bring it to us, that we may hear it and do it?" But the word is very near you. It is in your mouth and in your heart, so that **you can do it.*** (Deuteronomy 30:11-14, emphasis added)

You can do it!

APPENDIX: THE TRUTH AND AUTHORITY OF THE BIBLE

Historically, much as been written about the truth and authority of the Christian teaching contained in the Bible. While this teaching has been clarifying and helpful, it has also been exploited to disunify the followers of Jesus. Therefore, it is important to revisit this discussion using new words that may not have the same disunifying effect. The purpose of this chapter is to summarize what teaching followers of Jesus may conclude is true and authoritative.

I accept the Christian Bible (containing 66 books; 39 in the Old Testament and 27 in the New Testament) as 100% true and 100% authoritative.

By "true" I mean containing meaning that is absolute and real and which precedes and does not depend on a person's understanding or acceptance of them.

By "authoritative" I mean containing power to give benefits if the message is received and followed and to bring pain if the message is rejected.

Let me explain how I have arrived at this understanding of the Christian Bible.

The message of Jesus about Himself contained primarily in the four Gospels of the New Testament (Matthew, Mark, Luke, and John) is self-authenticating. The depth and power of the teaching of Jesus about Himself and His purpose, if received, are transformative and life-changing. In fact, Jesus Himself said that personal transformation (rebirth) is necessary to see the Kingdom of God, which is the purpose that Jesus said that He came to fulfill. Transformation is both a prerequisite for and a result of accepting, trusting in, and treasuring Jesus.

The message of Jesus is so radical, counter-intuitive, cosmic, and compelling that it stands on its own.

Having accepted the message and teaching of Jesus, the next logical step in answering the question "What Christian teaching is ultimately authoritative and true?" is to evaluate the rest of the Christian Bible, upheld for thousands of years by millions of people as being true and authoritative.

Jesus spoke extensively about the teaching of the Old Testament (the 39 books of the Christian Bible that precede the Gospels at the beginning of the New Testament). Most commonly, He referred to them as the Law and the Prophets. Technically, only a subset of the Old Testament is Law (the first 5 books of the Old Testament), and only a subset of the Old Testament is Prophets (the last 17 books of the Old Testament). There are 17 other books of the Old Testament that are left over to complete the full 39-book set, and these are commonly called the History and Wisdom books. They include well known Wisdom books such as Psalms and Proverbs and well-known History books such as Joshua, Judges, Ruth, and Esther.

The 39 books of the Old Testament were written and became widely accepted by the Hebrew people of Israel as a cohesive unit many years prior to the birth of Jesus. Therefore, when Jesus referred to the Law and the Prophets (and the Psalms, as in Luke 24:44), He was generally referring to the entire body of writing in the Old Testament.

Jesus unequivocally validated the authority and truth of the Old Testament writings as being divinely-inspired and as being about Him. He said in John 5:39 that it is the Scriptures (Old Testament writings) "that bear witness about me" and in John 5:46-47 "...if you believed Moses, you would believe me; for he wrote of me. But if you do not believe his writings, how will you believe my words?"

A close examination of the teaching of the Old Testament reveals a deep longing and anticipation of a coming Deliverer that will bring justice, healing, gladness, peace, and love with the establishment of His eternal kingdom for those who trust in God without wavering. The message of the Old Testament is not inconsistent with the teaching of Jesus, and the life of Jesus was shown by Jesus Himself to be the fulfilment of the Old Testament teaching and prophecies.

So, I accept the Old Testament as authoritative and true on the basis of Jesus' teaching.

The rest of the Christian New Testament, which includes the 23 books following the Gospels (beginning with the book of Acts and ending with Revelation) is primarily composed of letters written by early church leaders following the death of Jesus. The book of Acts is about the historical events of the early church that followed the death of Jesus, and the book of Revelation is a book of prophecy about the return of Jesus to the earth.

The New Testament was written almost entirely by eyewitnesses and close friends of Jesus. This has been established through an examination of other writings outside the Christian Bible that speak of the authorship of New Testament letters, and it is self-evident when examining the New Testament writings themselves, which read clearly as eyewitness accounts.

Even more important than the historical authorship of the New Testament letters is their message. Uniformly, the 23 remaining books of the New Testament validate Jesus as being Who He said He was (the God-Man Savior of all people who choose to receive and trust in Him alone) and exalt Him as supremely valuable, above all other causes and purposes.

So, stepping back from the discussion, I have come to see the Christian Bible as containing a single, cohesive message of ultimate hope and purpose that is centered on Jesus as the supreme protagonist of history. Though the Bible was written by many different men that lived at different times and wrote in different languages, its message is remarkably consistent. There are no meaningful inconsistencies.

In light of this, I have considered whether this single cohesive message is compelling and desirable. Do I accept Jesus? Do I trust Jesus? Can I treasure Jesus above everything else? Do I need Him?

Unequivocally, my answer is a resounding yes! On some days, I answer weakly, because of my internal battle against sin (which the Bible teaches will not be over until my physical body dies and I go to be with Jesus face to face forever). Nevertheless, my desire for Jesus has continued to grow and deepen in my life. I want to be with Him forever.

Before we leave the topic of authoritative Christian teaching about Jesus, a few other very valid questions should be asked and answered.

What about the various translations of the Bible (of which there are hundreds in the English language alone), and what about other writings such as the apocryphal or deuterocanonical writings which have been accepted by some Christian traditions (Roman Catholic and Greek and Russian Orthodox traditions) as authoritative but are not included in the 66 books of the Bible mentioned above? Should all translations and these additional writings be considered equally authoritative and true?

Before I answer this, it is important to answer a different question. What is the essence of the truth and authority found in the Christian teaching about Jesus?

Is the essence of the truth and authority found in the correct word choices and ordering of words within the writings? Is the essence of the truth and authority found in the correct selection of the books which are true and authoritative and the appropriate discarding of other books which are not true and authoritative? Where does the truth and the authority come from?

Here is my answer: The essence of the truth and authority found in the Christian teaching about Jesus is the *source* of the teaching and the *central message* of the teaching. The source is what validates the truth and gives it authority. The central message is the truth itself. The source of the teaching is God Himself. The Bible teaches that God's Spirit inspired the writing of the Old and New Testament authors. The central message is that *Jesus Christ is the supremely valuable God-Man that is infinitely beautiful and infinitely necessary for every single human being to have the deepest desires of his heart satisfied. Human beings cannot experience satisfaction of the deepest desires of their hearts apart from Jesus. This is true because every human being has a deep and pervasive problem with himself called sin which cannot be overcome apart from accepting, trusting in, and treasuring the work of Jesus on his behalf. Accepting, trusting in, and treasuring Jesus includes agreeing that Jesus is worth giving my life and everything I own away for His sake.*

Therefore, I can accept multiple translations of the Bible because the truth and authority do not come from correct word selection but from the divinely-inspired central message of the Bible about Jesus. I can also accept writing outside the Bible as true and authoritative if it is consistent with the teaching found in the 66 books of the Christian Bible. However, I am not compelled to accept writing outside the 66 books of the Christian Bible because the 66 books contain all that I need to understand and know about Jesus. They contain the central message about Him.

I have not read the apocryphal books (Tobit, Judith, Maccabees, Esdras, and other wisdom and prophetic books), but I would be glad to read them and to have a dialogue about their messages. I am not opposed to reading them, and I am not avoiding reading them. I simply do not feel compelled to read them. The 66 books of the Christian Bible stand on their own authority and truth without any meaningful deficiency.

A final word about Bible translations. While I said above that I can accept multiple translations of the Bible because the truth and authority of the Bible doesn't come from correct word selection but from the divinely-inspired central message of the Bible about Jesus, it is important to note the method, intention, and resources of the translator when reading any given translation.

For example, some translations were written in order to preserve as closely as possible the word ordering of the historical manuscripts in Hebrew and Greek, while others have taken a looser approach of maintaining the ordering of sentences and phrases but re-ordering the words within the sentences and phrases in order to increase readability, and still others may more accurately be described as paraphrased translations than as literal translations. Because God (authority) chose to give us the central message about Jesus (truth)

Who Am I?

in the form of a collection of writings using different languages, cultures, and time periods, reading and studying the writings as closely as possible to the original language and culture in which they were written is very valuable because it helps with preserving the full meaning and helps to enhance the beauty of the central message of Jesus. However, paraphrases such as the Message Bible are very valuable as well in using present-day metaphors and language to unpack the central message of Jesus.

Bible excerpts in this book are all from the English Standard Version (ESV) of the Bible. According to the ESV website (www.esv.org), "The ESV is an "essentially literal" translation that seeks as far as possible to capture the precise wording of the original text and the personal style of each Bible writer. As such, its emphasis is on "word-for-word" correspondence, at the same time taking into account differences of grammar, syntax, and idiom between current literary English and the original languages. Thus it seeks to be transparent to the original text, letting the reader see as directly as possible the structure and meaning of the original."

The ESV is the version of the Bible I use regularly, but I appreciate many others as well.

REFLECTION

He is the image of the invisible God, the firstborn of all creation. For by him all things were created, in heaven and on earth, visible and invisible, whether thrones or dominions or rulers or authorities—all things were created through him and for him. And he is before all things, and in him all things hold together. And he is the head of the body, the church. He is the beginning, the firstborn from the dead, that in everything he might be preeminent. For in him all the fullness of God was pleased to dwell, and through him to reconcile to himself all things, whether on earth or in heaven, making peace by the blood of his cross. (Colossians 1:15-20)

Long ago, at many times and in many ways, God spoke to our fathers by the prophets, but in these last days he has spoken to us by his Son, whom he appointed the heir of all things, through whom also he created the world. He is the radiance of the glory of God and the exact imprint of his nature, and he upholds the universe by the word of his power. After making purification for sins, he sat down at the right hand of the Majesty on high, having become as much superior to angels as the name he has inherited is more excellent than theirs. (Hebrews 1:1-4)

The true light, which gives light to everyone, was coming into the world. He was in the world, and the world was made through him, yet the world did not know him. He came to his own, and his own people did not receive him. But to all who did receive him, who believed in his name, he gave the right to become children of God, who were born, not of blood nor of the will of the flesh nor of the will of man, but of God. And the Word became flesh and dwelt among us, and we have seen his glory, glory as of the only Son from the Father, full of grace and truth.... For from his fullness we have all received, grace upon grace. (John 1:9-14,16)

LET US TALK

I would like to have a conversation with you about the message in this book. I would like to hear your thoughts. If I have said anything unhelpful or untrue, please extend grace to me and overlook what I have said if it is untrue or the manner in which I have said it if it is unhelpful. Please come and give me your feedback.

My email is wimcodington@gmail. My cell phone is 423.505.6411. I live in Nashville, TN. Let us dialogue together about the message of this book.

[1] See Maslow's article entitled "A Theory of Human Motivation" published in the *Psychological Review* scientific journal in 1943.

[2] This book contains extensive excerpts from the Bible. I accept the Bible as 100% true and 100% authoritative. I have explained why this is the case in an appendix to this book entitled "The Truth and Authority of the Bible."

[3] See Romans 11:17-24 for Paul's use of this metaphor of grafting branches into a tree.

[4] While unhealthy fears do not come from God, they can tell us about ourselves and our God-given wiring because people with certain temperaments are prone to certain fears, etc.

[5] Rick Warren, spoken at the Finishing the Task Conference in December 2018 at Saddleback Church in Lake Forest, CA.

[6] Exodus 15:26

[7] 2 Kings 20:8-11; Joshua 10:12-14; Judges 6:36-40; 2 Kings 4:1-7; John 11:1-44

[8] Isaiah 55:8-9

[9] Romans 11:33-34

Made in the USA
Lexington, KY
24 September 2019